Eat Right, Now!

RECIPES FOR A HEALTHY LIFESTYLE

CHEF WENDELL FOWLER

Guild Press
Emmis Publishing LP

Guild Press-Emmis Publishing, LP
10665 Andrade Drive
Zionsville, Indiana 46077

ISBN 1-57860-108-8
Library of Congress Catalog Card Number 20-02100566

Interior and text design by Sheila G. Samson

Back cover:
Photograph of Wendell Fowler by M.Photog., Craftsman
David A. Fowler, Fowler Photography, Ogallala, Nebraska

To Mutti,
> for her unconditional love and gentle spirit, and for
> tenderly nudging me down the right path,

and my wonderful wife, Sandi,
> for her love, support, and patience,

and finally, to my Creator,
> for His love, gifts, and all that I have.

Let food be thy medicine, and let medicine be thy food.
> — Hippocrates, ca. 460–377 B.C.

Contents

Introduction

Each of us has the physical equivalent of a space suit. We are born into our own individual "earth suit"; it goes with us and serves us well through many years. We part company with it only when we ourselves depart. It stands to reason that each of us should cherish our personal earth suit, take maximum care of it, and not abuse this marvelous gift.

I almost ruined mine. It began early in the 1970s. I was a passionate chef in every stereotypical sense of the word: one hundred pounds overweight, sedentary, smoking Marlboros and pot, partying and drinking like a fish, eating anything and everything. Fat and sugar were their own food group for me, and, in general, I would say that I abused my gift, my earth suit or body, with Olympian panache.

My weakness or addiction was a cocktail composed of a jigger of low self-esteem and a shot of self-abuse, shaken, not stirred, and garnished with ignorance and guilt—a deadly libation. I'm aware that I'm not the only consumer of the poison of poor self-esteem and reckless selfishness.

Then it happened: the tap on the shoulder, or more appropriately, the body slam. It can happen to anyone. This was the moment of truth and a test of my strength of mind. Luckily, I love a good challenge.

My earth suit freaked out by being driven to its limits. A simple act such as crossing the street left me winded. Breathing became labored and I had to really focus on the next breath, or I would gasp for air. Every night as I lay in bed, I prayed that I would wake up in the morning. Something was truly not right, I had to admit.

After an appointment with my family physician, I was very gently informed that I should go directly to the emergency room. There I discovered my resting heart rate was a dangerous 155. I was also experiencing atrial fibrillation and congestive heart failure. Quarts of fluid had accumulated around my heart, all due to a nasty virus which decided to homestead in the lining of my flabby, unexercised, gelatinous heart.

The diagnosis: viral cardiomyopathy. Just one french fry and cocktail away from taking a long nap on the wrong side of the sod, I'd hit the wall like a bug hitting a windshield.

It took tumbling into the deepest, darkest hole, lined with divorce, bankruptcy, and alcoholism, and kissing the bottom of that pit to get my attention. But it worked gloriously. I was lucky. My coronary crisis was the best thing that ever happened to me.

Reality is lying alone on a hard gurney, staring at the ceiling in a cold cardiac unit, surrounded by masked strangers, beeping heart monitors, with tubes and needles coming out of every available orifice. I had been given the death sentence by several cardiologists and my family physician. A little voice in my gut kept repeating, "Wendell, you just don't get it." I was frightened, alone. My only perception was that I should be dead.

This is the time when my transformation began; the prospect of death can be rather motivating. As soon as the doctors informed me of my upcoming demise, instead of feeling sorry for myself, I laughed. Then I laughed some more, and more, and more till my sides split. The only healthy use for denial. Death was not an option. I, quite simply, was not gong to die. It was not an issue. Case closed.

My faith was strong, and it saw me through. I learned many lessons and one of them was that fear is the absence of faith. So, I had to face whatever the future was with courage.

"All right, now what do I do?" I mused. "Pray and make peace with my Maker, or strike a deal? Yeah, that's it, I'll make a deal with my Creator." My life in return for what?

The mission was revealed: "Now that I have your attention, learn to use food as medicine, be a role model, and lovingly share your knowledge with others."

As Jake of the Blues Brothers so eloquently put it in his thickest Chicago accent, "For the rest of my life, I'm on a mission from Gaad."

And what was that mission? This is how I saw it:

- To become a nutritional evangelist, dedicated to positively affecting and hopefully improving eating and lifestyle habits of my family, friends and the people whom I influence.
- To create a user-friendly learning tool, composed of simple, uncomplicated, no-nonsense facts, researched information, and advice provided by individual authorities and scholars in their fields: an earth suit maintenance guide for the nutritionally inept. To assist in healing the diseases of the earth and its inhabitants, one loving spoonful at a time.
- To use my highly visible position as a professional chef as a podium to rectify, rather than to perpetuate, the bad eating habits so deeply rooted in the McDonaldization of America.
- Most of all, to teach each person I come in contact with to revere his or her earth suit, the lifelong home of the ever-wandering soul.

I discovered that Hippocrates was right when, around 400 B.C., he said, "Let food be thy medicine and let medicine be thy food." As I looked at the problem before me, it seemed overwhelming at first. I saw a nation awash in greasy giantburgers, kids getting ever heavier with each year as they stuff on fries and Fritos, restaurants that serve appetizers of fried cheese sticks and fried everything else, and frozen-food cases full of processed dinners. All of this was daunting.

Still, as I slowly made my way back to health and a new life, what I learned showed me that the cause was important. We are in an epidemic of ill health caused by poor living: diabetes, heart disease, lung and breast cancer, fibromyalgia, obesity, and arthritis. All of these are profoundly affected by our choices. What we eat or don't eat, how we manage our environment, whether we exercise, how we indulge our needs for pleasuring—all of these can alter our bodies, minds, and spirits.

The reassuring fact I found was that we have the power to undo the damage. If we are in nutritional bankruptcy, we can pay off the creditors and start again. No one says the trip is easy. Aware eating is an evolution into common-sense living, but it is a paradigm change that works. The small choices you can employ at the beginning of this book can evolve into major, satisfying changes that will become natural ways of living and thinking. Eating right becomes a catalyst for all sorts of progress in life.

I've shared my method with thousands of others through my television show and syndicated column in papers across the country, and with those for whom I cater, including the "hard-core, hamburger-only cases" on National Basketball Association airplanes. This book does not contain a diet. It describes, rather, a disciplined, positive lifestyle that best promotes health. This healthy lifestyle is not riddled with guilt, but seasoned with moderation and blessed with pats on the back for a job well-done—regardless of how much of it you absorb and use.

Eat Right, Now! is my gift of knowledge to you. May it bless you the way it has me.

If this book is not a "diet book," it is not a cookbook or a lifestyle book either. It is a combination of all these. In it I share my deep convictions about the impact of proper eating on everyday life and health and about the eating crisis in America today.

Each chapter contains information and philosophy about eating and ill health, specific statistics and charts about eating-related disorders and methodology instructing you on how to eat right—at this very moment! Each chapter focuses on a food-related issue in America today, followed by recipes to give you information on how to eat correctly.

My methodology progresses through three phased eating options in this book, and purposely works up to my own proven "best" eating for health option: vegetarianism. The first chapter shows how to take gradual steps towards improved eating habits, by making small changes in daily eating and in menu preparation. Since this is a health and fitness cookbook, too, recipes for delicious dishes that are variants of favorites are included at the end of the first chapter, with "light" and "lowfat" alterations made to improve nutrition without sacrificing flavor.

The next chapters emphasize choosing a specific dietary plan such as outlined by the USDA Food Pyramid, or better yet, the Mediterranean diet. Chapters on salads, luncheon dishes, vegetables, and pasta show how these products contribute to health and offer you nonvegetarian and vegetarian choices in recipes. Finally, following the traditional cookbook groupings of food, we proceed to entrées, and here you will find both nonvegetarian and vegetarian offerings. The chapter on desserts discusses sugars and sweetening products and then gives recipes for classic and light-eating desserts.

I do not hide the fact that I am convinced vegetarianism is the path to healthy living, so don't be shocked at the strong arguments I present, the quotations I include from vegetarian eaters and the sometimes shocking statistics and reports about the food industry.

I hope to make a case for sound nutrition and at the same time let you enjoy that good nutrition with good taste and fun and even a little inspiration for your family. Along the way, I'll be sharing some of the anecdotes and fun I've had through some thirty years in the food preparation industry.

I'm Wendell, and I'll be your server. Enjoy your meal!

CHAPTER ONE

Start With Fresh, Wholesome Food and Make Small Changes

The easiest way to get started on eating right, to improve the condition of your earth suit, is to study good nutrition and make small changes in your eating habits. Don't wait until you reach the point of crisis or even until next New Year's when you make resolutions—start today!

Begin with fresh, wholesome food. You'll discover this commitment begins in the grocery store. Let me walk you through it. You're entering the supermarket and the first section that greets you is the prepared-food deli. Walk right past that, tempting as it is, with all of those alfredo and au gratin potato dishes ready to pop into the micro. Nope. Turn into the fresh fruit and vegetable department. Doesn't it look delicious? Load these items into your cart, and try to find them in the organic food section if you can, where they've been picked vine and tree-ripe. Go for the asparagus, green beans, brussels sprouts, fresh leafy green vegetables, oranges, organically raised apples. Be sure to pick your favorites; let's celebrate the taste of the fresh food that will help revitalize your life.

Go very, very easy on the meats. Instead, there may be good, fresh fish there on ice. Choose that. We'll talk about the meat later. Walk briskly—or waddle—past the bakery section, pausing only at the seven-grain bread stand. Leave the cream pies and crumb cakes for somebody less disciplined than the new you.

And as for the freezer section, loaded with macaroni and cheese, gravy-laden dinners-to-go, pies, and sweetrolls—just pass it by.

The food you keep in your kitchen is what you are going to eat, so plan your grocery shopping and buy only wholesome, unprocessed fresh foods, low in sugar. Minimize meat, and maximize vegetables, fruits, and whole grains. Now you're talking! No matter how you fix them, these foods are a big improvement over the gooey goodies you may have chosen before.

Now that you have your cart full of fresh (and hopefully organic) vegetables and fruit and a little fish and meat, here are some kitchen strategies for starting to eat better:

- Nonstick, nonstick, nonstick! Use a nonstick surface and you don't need shortening or butter to sauté or sear your meat or fish. And the food's natural juices will help to cook your piece of meat or fish in a much more savory way.
- Look at the plate you are preparing for supper. Increase the portions of vegetables you're putting on it, decrease the portion of meat or fish or chicken to the size of the palm of your hand. As an experiment, try an all-vegetarian dinner, and use broth or garlic instead of butter for the mashed potatoes, which can be the "main dish."
- Use a wide variety of vegetables your family likes or is willing to try. Remember, not every vegetable has to be peas or green beans. Acorn squash, sweet potatoes, kale, limas, okra, artichokes, spinach, beets—all are delicious. Be nutritionally adventurous.
- Steam those vegetables, cut the salt to nothing, and use pepper instead to flavor. Eliminate the butter. When you can, choose olive oil in cooking instead of butter and avoid margarine.
- Substitute whole-grain bread, bran muffins, pitas, and brown rice for white products.
- When making soup or saving stock for gravy, skim all the fat off or, better yet, refrigerate the strained broth so the fat will rise to the top.

Look at all your recipes to see how you can eliminate or cut fat, mayonnaise, sugar, rich cheese, salt and whole milk.

After a while you may be ready for a disciplined diet change.

One well-known dietary plan is based on the USDA Food Pyramid. Some people believe this plan has flaws because it was influenced by the food industries. Still, in fairness, the basic food pyramid is an improvement over the fast-food-lunch and freezer-dinner approach too many Americans have adopted.

I asked an expert from Community Hospital East in Indianapolis to share with us her recommendations for a heart-healthy diet based on the USDA Food Pyramid. Here is her letter of advice:

Dear Wendell:

The United States Department of Agriculture (USDA) developed the Food Pyramid in 1996 to help Americans eat a balanced, healthy diet. They recommend [daily] 6–11 servings of breads and grains, 3–5 servings of vegetables, 2–4 servings of fruits; 2–3 servings of milk, yogurt, and cheese; 2–3 servings of meat, poultry, or fish; and sparse use of alcohol, sweets, salt, fats, and oils.

But what about portion size? What is a serving? Specific examples provided by the USDA include:

A serving of grains, bread, or rice is one slice of bread, one cup of cereal, $1/2$ cup of cooked cereal and rice (try to use whole grain such as brown rice, whole grain corn, oatmeal, barley, popcorn, whole oats, rye, and wheat).

Vegetable serving equals one cup of leafy vegetables, $1/2$ cup of cooked or raw vegetables or vegetable juice.

Fruit serving equals one medium apple, banana, orange, pear, $1/2$ cup of chopped, cooked, or canned fruit, $3/4$ cup of fruit juice.

Milk, yogurt, cheese group serving equals one cup of milk or yogurt, $1^1/2$ ounces of natural cheese such as cheddar, and 2 ounces of processed cheese such as American (choose nonfat or reduced-fat dairy products most often).

Meat, poultry, fish, dry beans, eggs, and nuts group (meat

and beans group) serving size equals 2–3 ounces of cooked lean meat, poultry, or fish. An ounce of lean meat is equivalent to $1/2$ cup of cooked dry beans, $1/2$ cup of tofu (soybean curd), a $2^1/2$-ounce soyburger, 1 egg, 2 tablespoons of peanut butter, or $1/3$ cup of nuts.

The USDA Food Pyramid is used to base a diet which is good for the heart—the Heart Healthy Diet.

The Heart Healthy Diet reduces the risk of hypertension, obesity and atherosclerosis with a subsequent decrease in risk of stroke (American Heart Association, 2001). What is a heart healthy diet? According to the American Heart Association:

- A diet that includes a variety of fruits and vegetables (five servings per day).
- Grain products—particularly whole-grain products (six or more servings per day).
- Low-fat dairy products, fish, skinless poultry, and lean meats.
- Limited use of saturated fats, trans-fatty acids and/or cholesterol (people with heart disease and/or high cholesterol should limit their saturated fats to less than 7 percent of calories and eat less than 200 mg of cholesterol per day), and 2400 mg of sodium a day.
- No more than one alcoholic drink a day if you are a woman and no more than two if you are a man. (One drink is equal to 12 ounces of beer, 4 ounces of wine and $1^1/2$ ounces of 80 proof spirits or 1 ounce of 100 proof spirits.)
- The number of calories in your daily diet should be balanced with the number of calories burned or used in a day (multiply your [ideal] weight in pounds by 15 if you are moderately active or by 13 if you get little exercise).

— Marsha S. Meckel, R.N., B.S.N.
Community Hospitals, Indianapolis

The descriptions of the Mediterranean as presented by Homer, Van Gogh, Matisse, and Picasso evoke images of sparkling deep blue water against light blue skies and sun-drenched farmlands, fishing villages, olive groves, vineyards, and farmer's markets bursting with seasonal harvests.

This magnificent sea region gave birth to the Mediterranean diet some 2000 years ago in Bible times. Many refer to it as the Bible diet.

After a while you may be ready for this best of the disciplined diet changes. I believe it is an improvement over the USDA Food Pyramid plan.

The diet that people followed in biblical times is still being followed in that region of the world. It is long meals, not fast food; it is fresh, not frozen, and it is a diet long on soluble and insoluble fiber, antioxidants, phytonutrients and many all-important nutrients often deficient in the American diet.

The Mediterranean diet is based on a well-documented historical and environmental reality. People around the Mediterranean Sea ate olives, grains, and flat bread and hard cheese and grapes because that's what grew there and was easily available. They cooked and dressed their salads with olive oil because the trees were everywhere. But we now know that the food-choice pyramid they observed is compatible with excellent health. It has taken 2000 years, however, to really define itself.

Prominent scientists recently conceded that the Mediterranean diet is healthier than the American diet because more grains, fruits, vegetables, legumes, nuts, and olive oil are consumed. The biggest difference is that red meat is much less emphasized in the Mediterranean diet pyramid, compared to the American diet in general, with beef, pork, cheese, and yogurt, along with eggs, poultry, and fish comprising the predominant sources of protein. Generally, in America, meat is the center of the plate, and apparently the more the better.

Eating red meat is not necessarily macho and it isn't necessary for health. The Mediterranean diet promotes 12–15 ounces of red meat per month, not per meal; the Bible diet also states that red meat is to be eaten only once a month and only for a special celebration. In 1998 the total U.S. consumption of meat (including red meat, poultry, and fish) was estimated at 196 pounds per person. That is six pounds more than in the previous year, and nineteen pounds above the 1970 level, according to the United States Department of Agriculture. It may be that this increase in meat consumption is a result of our hurried lifestyle, which depends on quick food meals.

The Mediterranean diet, on the other hand, is based upon a laid-back lifestyle that includes exercise, pleasure, and leisure. It seems as though Midwesterners are so time-strapped that they have no time for a communal family dinner. As a result, we wolf down three squares a day at the most conveniently placed fast food drive-through and harden the collective arteries of the entire family. Not so in wine and olive country, where long evenings include these good simple foods and lots of companionable talk.

Interest in the lifestyle of the Mediterranean area, often called the Cradle of Civilization, began in the 1950s, at a time when health officials' concerns about diet and its role in chronic diseases were on the upswing. Studies began in Naples, Italy, where, despite high intakes of fat (mostly from olive oil), citizens had a very low rate of morbidity and mortality from coronary disease. The studies spread to other countries in southern Europe—Spain, Greece, and France—where their citizens' diets were compared to those of northern European countries and those of North America.

The studies broadened and began focusing on the type of oils used for cooking, and of course olive oil won the debate hands down.

Olive oil is a friendly fat or, scientifically speaking, a mono-unsaturated fat. In his book *Fats That Heal, Fats That Kill*, Udo Erasmus states that "monounsaturated fatty acid-rich virgin olive oil has been shown to reduce the production of cholesterol gallstones (compared to high-polyunsaturated, refined corn oil), and to favor bile secretion, which improves elimination of the toxic end products of liver detoxification and improves digestion of fats." In addition, as a chef, I've observed that extra virgin, first cold-pressed olive oil has an ethereal, fruity flavor which would turn any dish into a plate fit for an emperor.

Extra virgin olive oil makes a delicious salad dressing when mixed with red wine vinegar, lots of raw garlic, sea salt, cracked pepper, and a smidgen of Dijon mustard. However, I gently advise you to take care when cooking with extra virgin olive oil, for cooking destroys the delicately fruity essence for which it is renowned. Use a more all-purpose olive oil for cooking and frying.

Perhaps someone will open a true Mediterranean fast-food place and do us all a favor. In the meantime, we need to stop driving through these grease factories for the mouth that now exist. Speed isn't everything.

To do that, we need to change our perception of food and "eat to live, rather than live to eat." I have noticed that there are two types of eaters: conscious and unconscious, with unconscious eaters putting whatever occurs to them in their mouths without regard for its nutritional content. They are eating for the sake of eating, with little or no regard for balance or nutrient content. I believe food must be celebrated and perceived as more than something you put into your body in order to stay alive. Healing begins at the dinner table. Food is medicine, and every spoonful counts toward a higher, more fulfilling quality of life. Our bodies are one big biochemical factory, and what we put in them has a remarkable effect on how we feel at this very moment and the status of our health twenty years from now.

Sometimes it takes an outsider to clearly see specific problems in a culture. Canadian nutritionist Pascale Messier, B.S., a dietitian and exercise physiologist at the National Institute for Fitness and Sport (NIFS), moved from Ottawa to Indianapolis in 2001. She was amazed to see the disturbing proliferation of fast-food outlets, how constantly busy they were, and how many of the diners there were dangerously overweight.

"This was a real eye opener for me," she said. "Now I understand why Indiana is one of the fattest states in America." Pascale had never heard of Arby's, Steak 'n Shake, or White Castle before she moved here. She said that should could not recall fast-food restaurants being this busy back home, where, she states, portions are much smaller. She remembers vividly her first meal in Indy, sitting on a restaurant terrace next to a family of overweight children with greasy, super-sized plates loaded with food before them. More is not necessarily better. This fad of super-sizing just about everything an American has, according to recent reports, resulted in an increase of atherosclerosis and cholesterol levels in preteens as well as in mature adults. Could this be one of the reasons 60 percent or so of Midwesterners are grossly overweight?

Our motto seems to be roll out of your car, roll into a booth, pig out, burp, and then roll back out of the restaurant, roll into the car then roll into bed. Or better yet, don't even get out of the car.

I urge you to take a good look at your lifestyle, slow down, smell the daffodils and lilies. Park a little farther from the grocery store or restaurant when you go out to enjoy food. That extra block or two hiking to the cafe will stimulate you. Consciously watch what you eat at that restaurant and try the change-choices suggested in this chapter. And finally, pat yourself on the back for taking that first step toward optimum health.

After eating at home, take the family and the dog for a bond-strengthening, sunset walk. You'll find that sniffing those spring daffodils as a family makes them smell even better.

And, most of all, look carefully at the recipes you've always enjoyed cooking. How can you make them lighter and more healthful? Perhaps even, and finally, you may wish to vegetarianize your life. I'll try to convince you to do just that later in the book. For now, though, you can move right into better eating for health and flavor and improve your earth suit with definitive decisions.

With a little knowledge, you can eat right now and right away!

Here's a little knowledge:

- A broccoli and tofu stir-fry contains more calcium than one cup of milk or one cup of steamed spinach. Consider skipping meat when you can.
- Eating a plant-based diet can reduce your risk for hypertension and heart disease, Type 2 diabetes, lung and colon cancer, kidney disease, and obesity. Think about it.
- For women, one hour a week of walking can cut the risk of heart disease, perhaps by as much as a half. Choose thirty minutes of walking instead of a TV show after supper.
- Take your lunch to work.

- For brown bag lunches choose celery, broccoli, and carrot sticks and/or pretzels instead of potato chips; a bottle of water or tea instead of soda, a natural peanut butter sandwich on whole grain bread, or a salad with a small amount of dressing in the side of the container. And at the restaurant with the gang, try broiled anything instead of fried, salad instead of sandwich, clear soup instead of cream soup.
- The term vegetarian was not even coined until the Bible Christian Church established the British Vegetarian Society in the 1840s. Pythagoras, however, was touting a vegetable diet as a necessity for both physical and spiritual needs twenty-five hundred years ago. This is not a new fad!
- Restaurant menu items which are likely to be made with animal products include: refried beans, bean soups, and french fries (lard); Caesar salads (anchovies and raw egg); biscuits, pie crusts, and cakes (shortening); mousses and gelatins (hooves of animals); and stir-fries (little bits of meat used for flavoring). Pass them by.
- McDonald's french fries contain artery-clogging trans-fats. Choose the salad if you must visit a fast-food place.
- Vegetarians have longer, healthier lifespans than their carnivorous counterparts. Vegetarians can live, on average, a full ten to fifteen years longer than meat eaters. Consider vegetarianzing your diet to the greatest extent possible. Be sure you get enough protein if you go vegetable.
- Soy milk has absolutely no cholesterol. Soy milk is digestible by lactose-intolerant persons. It's also lower in saturated fat and higher in B vitamins than cow's milk. Would you be venturesome enough to give it a try?
- The *American Journal of Clinical Nutrition* has shown that vegetarians have the edge on meat eaters in staying slender. You just need to keep the fatty foods to a minimum. Consider eating right for weight loss.
- Fish generally contains the highest levels of toxic chemicals. Still, it's better for you than meat.
- Seventy-five million Americans become ill each year from

contaminated food. Ask questions in restaurants and do
return food if you taste bleach or other strange flavors.

- Vitamins A, E, and C provide antioxidant protection against
  cell damage that causes your body to age. Read labels and
  grow vitamin-conscious.
- If you're over sixty-five years old, too much protein can
  increase the wear and tear on your kidneys. Avoid fad diets.
- Marjoram, peppermint, and rosemary help to slow aging.
  Research the benefits of herbs.

*Your choice of diet can influence your long-term
health prospects more than any other action you
might take.*

— C. Everett Koop
Former Surgeon General

Many healthy substitutions for foods you commonly use are readily available in most grocery stores. You may want to consider them as you cook.

Instead of:	Try:
Bacon	Canadian bacon, turkey bacon, or soy "bacon" bits.
Ground Beef	Ground turkey, chicken, buffalo, or venison. (Rudolph, is that you?)
Butter	Olive oil, nonhydrogenated vegetable oils, and pressed vegetable oils, or equal parts applesauce or equal parts prune purée for baking. (Try saying "prune purée" three times, real fast.) If you must cook with butter, cut back by one-third.
Cooking oils	Equal parts applesauce, puréed prunes, or puréed bananas.
Sautéing oils	Apple juice, sherry, vegetable stock, or wine.
Salad dressings	Citrus juices or cider vinegar thickened with puréed roasted red peppers, carrots, onions, or garlic.
Chocolate	Carob chips or Dutch processed cocoa.
Gelatin	Agar-agar, arrowroot, ground nuts and seeds, xantham gum, or kudzu, a starchy powder from a tropical tuber.
Sugar	Stevia powder, Sucanat, honey, or maple syrup. If you absolutely must bake with processed sugar, then cut back by one-third. You will need to increase the liquid by one-fourth. If the batter is too stiff, add a drop or two of liquid. To enhance the flavor when sugar is reduced, add vanilla, cinnamon, or nutmeg. Aspartame doesn't work, plus it's toxic to our systems.
Cream cheese	Yogurt cheese, nonfat cream cheese, or domestically produced Neufchâtel cheese. Yogurt cheese can be made by placing a container of plain yogurt into a cheesecloth-lined strainer, then leaving it overnight to drain. A delicious treat.

Instead of:	Try:
Cottage or ricotta cheese	Crumbled tofu
Pound cake	Angel food cake
Coconut milk	1 cup nonfat plain organic yogurt, $1/2$ cup nonfat milk, and $1/2$ teaspoon coconut extract.
Cookies	Meringue cookies, gingersnaps, sugar wafers, animal crackers, fig bars, graham crackers, or vanilla wafers. Read the labels and be alert to the ingredients. Many cookies contain dangerous trans-fats, or hydrogenated or partially hydrogenated oils.
Cheese	Vegetarian Grace Slick of the Jefferson Starship once referred to cheese as "liquid meat." She is correct, for dairy cheese products contain animal fats. Substitute low-fat versions or soy cheese, and use hard grating cheeses like Parmesan or Romano. There are some wonderful soy cheeses available in grocery stores.
Breadcrumbs	Toasted wheat germ or stale French bread. Simply process with a blender or food processor, but back off on the butter and oils.
Heavy cream	Very cold evaporated milk. If you need whipped cream for a topping, try low-fat yogurt or buttermilk.
Créme fraîche	Low-fat or nonfat plain organic yogurt.
White sauce	Puréed white beans.
Flour *(for thickening)*	Cornstarch or arrowroot slurry.
Sour cream	Low-fat or nonfat sour cream, buttermilk, or low-fat organic yogurt.
Crackers	Melba toasts, flatbreads, lavosh, matzo, rice cakes, rice crackers, baked tortilla chips, or pita bread triangles.
Mayonnaise	Soy mayonnaise.
Eggs	Crumbled or puréed tofu

Now you know. So, make those small, significant changes in food and lifestyle that will lead to a better quality of life.

Making Small Changes Recipes

COOKING LIGHTER

Potato Casserole

This is a typical family recipe—a rich one—that can be reorganized for better health without affecting the flavor. (Recipe courtesy of Jeane W. Schlemmer of Carmel, Indiana)

6	medium potatoes
1/4	cup butter
1	can cream of mushroom soup
1 1/2	cups grated cheddar cheese
1	pint sour cream
1/3	cup chopped onions
1	cup cornflakes
3	tablespoons melted butter
	Salt and pepper

Microwave potatoes. Cool, peel, and grate.

In a large pan, heat the 1/4 cup butter with the soup. Blend in the cheese, sour cream, onions, and salt and pepper to taste. Mix in the potatoes then place in a greased 2-quart casserole dish.

Mix cornflakes with 3 tablespoons melted butter and sprinkle over the casserole. Bake at 350 degrees for 45 minutes or till golden.

Special note: This dish is a classic, and in the past I have been guilty of shoveling down several portions of this rich potato dish during a Thanksgiving dinner. However, it is loaded with animal fats and science has shown that these saturated fats can lead to heart disease and obesity. We also know that being overweight can lead to diabetes, joint stress, diminished quality of life, and certain kinds of cancer. What to do?

First, leave the skins on the cleaned and scrubbed potatoes for increased nutrition and fiber. Instead of microwaving and grating the spuds, dice or slice and boil them. We could further lighten this recipe by using nonfat sour cream and substituting olive oil for butter. Yes, this will affect the flavor, but not negatively. Next, I suggest using a low-fat cheddar or trying a low-fat soy cheese substitute. Plan a trip to your favorite health food store to purchase some low-sodium cream of mushroom soup. Finally, I advise not announcing before dinner that you have made something healthy—it's the kiss of death!

Broccoli and Cheese Casserole

The following is an altered version of a family favorite that shows how small changes get big results in lowering fat, sodium, and sugar. This ubiquitous dish has appeared on our Christmas dinner table since I was a child, and is absolutely delicious. However, the butter, sodium, and processed cheese traditionally used in its preparation make it a real bloater. Try this recipe and no one will know it's not the rich version.

2   cups converted brown rice
1   pound mushrooms, thoroughly cleaned
1   cup chopped onions
2   10-ounce packages frozen cut or chopped broccoli
2   10.75-ounce cans of low-sodium cream of mushroom soup
$\frac{1}{4}$ cup extra virgin olive oil or unhydrogenated vegetable oil
1   pound soy cheddar cheese, cut up, or grated low-fat cheddar
    Sea salt and pepper

Cook rice according to package directions. Sauté mushrooms and onions in scant amount of olive oil. Lightly blanch the broccoli and drain well.

Combine all ingredients and mix thoroughly. Season to taste with salt and pepper. Place mixture in a 9 x 13-inch casserole dish. Bake at 350 degrees for 35 minutes. Serves 12.

Now try a "small-changes," healthier version of the mashed potatoes your family loves —

Smashed Potatoes

2½   pounds Yukon Gold potatoes, unpeeled and cut in large dice
1   12-ounce container of organic soft silken tofu
1   tablespoon minced fresh garlic
¼   cup freshly chopped parsley
½   cup extra virgin olive oil
1   cup hot skim milk
   Sea salt and pepper

Cook the potatoes until they can easily be pierced with a fork. Drain and add the tofu, garlic, parsley, and olive oil. With an electric mixer, beat on low speed just till combined.

Add hot milk a little at a time until you've reached desired consistency. (Overwhipping makes the potatoes gummy, so don't overwhip unless you plan on doing some wallpapering.) Season with salt and pepper to taste and serve.

Special note: The addition of the tofu to this dish packs it with clean protein and cancer-fighting phytochemicals. Add some cooked, drained spinach or greens to this and you will have an Irish dish called colcannon. The greens also give the dish a calcium and vitamin K boost. What a lovely way to say "I love you" to your family. Bon appetit!

Now, let's get specific about right eating. We'll see how we can waltz our way through a traditional cookbook, section by section, with recipes for healthy living. And I hope you don't mind the philosophy behind them!

CHAPTER TWO

Appetizers and Hors d'oeuvres

As you make changes to improve your diet and your earth suit, and perhaps adopt a diet plan like the Mediterranean diet, you might as well start at the beginning of the meal.

Appetizers can either make or break the healthy diet program. These "first" foods are designed to whet the appetite, but if they are rich in themselves, they can substitute for the entire meal. Instead try moderation and make choices. A well-designed veggie tray can be nutritious and satisfying, and a fruit display with toothpicks to "pick and choose" from is satisfying food. If you are hostess, you may wish to Mediterranianize your appetizer tray with olive oil in attractive small bowls for dipping, with whole-wheat focaccia bread or pitas or slices of toasted, whole-wheat bagels. Delectable and great for you!

First we need to analyze when and how we eat appetizers. It's pretty obvious that this is not home food. We don't sit down at the kitchen table and wait for the cook to put shrimp cocktail before us. We eat appetizers when we eat out at restaurants and when we are invited to parties.

Let's talk first about choosing from the appetizer menu at restaurants. Even though today's hors d'oeuvres menus are heavy with dishes which do not enhance health (fried cheese, fried calamari, crab cakes) there are still good choices. My wife Sandi and I like to choose shrimp cocktails, but we always need to make sure the shrimp is cooked. Shrimp should not be translucent and raw looking, but pure white, and have a bit of "crunch" when you bite into them.

Sushi is popular, and though I'm uncomfortable with uncooked fish, many persons are willing to take the risk. Sushi is loaded with nutrients and certainly is a low-fat choice. You can choose an antipasto dish, salsa, anything with beans (hummus is perfect), bean dips, or lard-free Mexican dishes (but go easy on the cheese), crab or almost any kind of boiled or broiled seafood offering.

You may wish to order a salad as your appetizer. If so, best have them put the dressing on the side. That way you can use a small amount and spread it around the way you wish, getting the same flavor without that "drenched in dressing," too-rich taste with the load of calories that goes along with it. Plus, with all that dressing, it's hard to taste the vegetables.

Now let's talk about parties. Here are some suggestions for staying temperate at the gala events:

Best way to avoid stuffing your face: Don't go to the party hungry. Snack earlier in the day and select a bagel and nonfat cream cheese, nonfat yogurt, or low-fat muffin, and lots of water so you won't walk through the door feeling the need to attack the hors d'oeuvres.
Best way to avoid heartburn: Don't stuff your face. When you overeat and indulge in fatty foods, your poor, struggling stomach secretes strong digestive acids. When your stomach is overly full, these acids get squeezed upward into the esophagus, causing painful heartburn.

But if you do give in, here's the easiest way to burn off calories: After you're too stuffed and tired to move, drag your posterior off the recliner and go outside into the invigorating air and take a brisk walk. Just being outdoors will speed up your metabolism as your body begins to warm itself.

As a rule, to make small changes and regulate the rest of your life, you'll have to get to know what foods to avoid. Eggnog, Caesar salad, nacho and other rich cheeses, and cream sauces seem to do the most damage to our immune systems and our overall health. When you hit the buffet table, avoid the cheeses, whether as hot fondues or as little bitty squares on toothpicks. Waiters will circulate, of course, at posh events, bearing little trays of delicacies. Take one and pass the rest by. Pass by little sausages in bacon, mushrooms with cheese bubbling on top, pastry wraps with good things inside. You can see the shortening lying on the top of these cooked gems: it's hydrogenated and therefore a true no-no. Smile and say just say no, then head for the giant pile of fruits, vegetables, dips, and crackers in the middle of the table. You can eat almost to your heart's content there, even if you do isolate yourself a bit socially by standing and plucking strawberries out of the pile for five minutes. Way to go!

It seems as if appetizers and hors d'oeuvres are particularly on display during the holidays. I estimate that at the winter holidays, most of us indulge in 75 percent of the appetizer calories we may get for an entire year. That's when rich start-the-meal foods are also the most dangerous.

We're psychologically conditioned—face it. I love Christmas and Thanksgiving, but what I like even more are the weeks and days leading up to the celebrations. The music, goodwill, and get-togethers, and the time with the family, talking, sharing—and the glorious food—are all rewarding.

During the holiday we have access to foods that we don't normally eat a lot during the year. Candy, eggnog, desserts, gravy, potatoes, and drinks add up over time, leading to an annual bout with corpulent porkiness. And holiday appetizers, though they look small and dainty, can be as bad as any of the main-course foods.

Most of our eating habits over the holidays are powered by our strong emotional attachment for the traditional foods and associated smells that nurture us. Cozy, comforting cuisine is as much a holiday requisite as pine wreaths, flickering Bayberry candles, or glistening cups of eggnog enjoyed by the flickering fire.

All it takes to get me going is the sound of Bing Crosby's "White Christmas" or Burl Ives' "Holly Jolly Christmas," and I'm yearning for all the foods that I know darned well will compromise the integrity of my health and immune system. Unfortunately, we don't like to think about that until after the holidays are over and we no longer fit into those new slacks or suits and a notch has been added to our belts. Pounds are so easy and fun to put on, but so very difficult to remove.

We all know that steamed vegetables and brown rice can't hold their own on a buffet table already groaning with the weight of fat-laden, less Spartan delights. For the quintessential American holiday, we should first give thanks for our bounty and then celebrate the birth of Christ, or the Jewish holidays or Kwanza. These are at the center of the celebration. But food follows fast on that list of important holiday features.

And of course, at every table is the ubiquitous turkey at the center of the production. You lie awake all night fretting, "Will my turkey be moist? Will my stuffing have enough flavor? Will I ever learn how to make good gravy?" That's not what you should be worried about.

A typical Thanksgiving/Christmas feast generally contains about 2500 fat-filled calories, 140 grams of animal fat, and a whopping 120 grams of cholesterol. Perhaps that is where we begin to put on that extra ten pounds we usually pick up over the holidays. Even though the holidays bring out the best in people, there is still a dark side to them.

Here are helpful hints for facing the holidays, especially as you look at the groaning party boards:

- Lose ten pounds before the holidays begin (in your dreams—but what a good aspiration).
- Pump up on your multivitamins before and after you splurge. Research has indicated that taking natural, food-based forms of vitamins C, E, A, and sublingual B complex will help pass the cholesterol through your system without too much being retained.
- Peg Daly of Indianapolis, Indiana, and founder of the Complementary Medicine Practitioner, suggests taking L-carnitine, a free-form amino acid dietary supplement, to help reduce fat and cholesterol absorption.
- Remember that alcoholic drinks have a large number of calories. Let safety and moderation be your guide for a happy and low calorie season.
- Take an herbal extract of milk thistle when you imbibe alcoholic beverages because it's able to detoxify and it gives

the liver potent protection. When grazing at the buffet table, sample each food in conservative portions and stay away from the chips, nuts, dips, and cheese. Instead, opt for high-fiber foods, which will fill you up quicker. Practice moderation.

- We've already said it: If it's in a little fondue pot or chafing dish, walk in the opposite direction. If you succumb to one tiny, fat-laden delicacy, resist a second helping. Go for the crudités.
- Get enough sleep so you will have the strength to follow your normal eating habits. Being tired and over-stimulated can make it harder to follow your regular eating habits.
- Last, but not least, exercise. Exercise is an important part of weight control. It keeps your muscles fit, burns off calories, and reduces stress.

In recent years appetizers have become the staple food for entertaining. Whole parties are designed around them! As a caterer, I'm able to observe parties—successful and otherwise. I'd like to offer some suggestions here for your next event and I'd like to urge you to design a healthy as well as a festive board for your friends. Whether you have one of those appetizer-only parties or include other courses and treats, you can make food, fun, and health flow together. Here's a typical scenario for success. While I have the chance, I'll even throw in some catered-event planning tips. Be my guest. Or I'll be yours.

Entertaining at Home —

The "KIFF" Theory (Keep It Fuss-Free)

It takes a lot of planning and hard work to put together a memorable holiday soirée. Most often party-givers tend to make things more difficult than they need be, when they could be out enjoying themselves at their own party. Plan a menu based upon its degree of difficulty. Be practical. When you saw that TV chef prepare it the other day it sure looked easy, huh? Dumb it down a little.

Pick up a current holiday food magazine and newspapers to explore new culinary horizons. Make their recipes lighter in the ways we showed in the last chapter, eliminating fats, substituting less caloric ingredients for calorie-laden ones.

Plan the menu weeks in advance. Don't be too fussy; one main entrée is sufficient. Prepare what you can, like casseroles, and freeze them in advance. Have a layout diagram for the buffet table, and then set the table up the day before. Consider table decorations, but avoid heavily scented candles, for they will unfavorably overpower the mouth-watering aroma of the delicious morsels you slaved over all week.

When considerate guests ask you what they can contribute, suggest wine, sparkling water, homemade bread, or a special dessert. They can contribute "light" too!

And there are more ways to Eat Right, Now! with appetizers at parties. Purchase a domestic cheese or veggie tray at the local grocery store. To the veggie tray, add some pepperoncini peppers, deviled eggs, marinated olives, blanched asparagus, and some wedges of blanched, then grilled, baby Yukon Gold potatoes to schmaltz the tray up a bit and convert it into an antipasto salad. Little pieces of diced summer sausage, Dijon mustard, strawberries and grapes, and stalks of fresh rosemary will perk up the otherwise predictable cubed-cheese tray presentation from the grocery store. Simple and nutritious. (For even better health, I, of course, suggest eliminating the summer sausage.)

Several trays can be placed around the house, always conveniently accessible to your guests between trips to and from the food buffet or bar. Consider placing bowls of your famous homemade Chex-mix or spiced nuts on the bar for a quick, convenient munch.

Toss out your "war horse" recipes and opt for some new, unpredictable and refreshingly new ideas this season. How many times can you eat chicken liver rumaki, buffalo wings, and mini-quiche without gagging? And if I never see another spinach dip, it will be too soon. The surprisingly flavorful, low-fat Pickled Ginger Dip recipe in the recipe section (page 25) will have your guests guessing and raving. Try it as a dip for vegetables—then sit back and enjoy the compliments.

Use small cocktail plates so your guests will have to frequent the buffet table more often, and when you plan the layout and flow of the party, keep the food table and the bar as far away from each other as possible. These two strategies will force your guests to mingle more often, therefore resulting in a more successful party.

Remember, how you word the invitation will dictate your guests' expectations. Is it a full-blown dinner, open house, heavy or light hors d'oeuvres, snacks only, or pastries and tea? If you have a lighter budget, schedule the affair in the afternoon, and guests will not expect a meal.

And the small plates and light appealing fare may encourage your special guests to eat lighter and more healthfully.

MORE SUGGESTIONS FOR KEEPING YOUR PARTY SIMPLE AND STRESS-FREE:

- Set the table a few days in advance so you'll have plenty of time to balance, fill in, and replace so the table is perfect. Add crystal glasses the day of the party.
- Elevate some foods on the buffet table. (Make light foods prominent.)
- Throughout the house, lighten up. Small, flickering votive candles create a magical, enchanting holiday mood.
- Use smaller floral arrangements instead of centerpieces that can overpower the table and block guests' view.
- Pre-fold the napkins. Teach yourself a new way to fold the napkins and surprise your guests.
- Work in advance. Seventy-five percent of all party food can be prepared early, but be sure you refrigerate correctly. Food must be kept at 41 degrees or lower.
- If you are serving a turkey, cook it the day before, let it cool, then carve and refrigerate the meat. When it's party time, reheat the meat, covered, at 275 degrees to an internal temperature of 160 degrees. It's a real stress buster—that, and a sparkling glass of wine.
- Most holiday dishes include a vegetable as an afterthought in the form of a garnish. Increase proportions of the broccoli or asparagus in your casserole dishes, and be sure plenty of fresh, unadorned, blanched veggies are available.
- Holiday fare is heavy on cheese and cream. Use skinny versions of dairy ingredients—or better yet, stick to dairy-free alternatives. Soy cheese, anyone?
- Butter is the biggest offender, and can easily be cut by half in most recipes. From bread to soups, use healthier oils, like olive or nonhydrogenated vegetable oils. An unhydrogenated vegetable nonstick spray is an acceptable alternative for sautéeing. Again, more is not better.

Eat Right Recipes

APPETIZERS

Holiday Vegetarian Eggnog

We've successfully served this delicious version of eggnog over the years, and you'd be hard pressed to tell the difference. The creamy, protein-packed holiday beverage has the same rich, creamy, buttery, and full-flavored feel as the overly fatty traditional beverage. Most often, we'll make a pitcher and offer it to our guests without telling how it was made. After the glowing warm compliments begin coming in, we tell them our secret. The jaws drop, the lips smack, and you hear, "May I have another glass?"

3/4   cup vanilla soy or rice milk
4   teaspoons vanilla
2   10-ounce packages organic soft silken tofu
1/3   cup Sucanat (Or brown sugar, if you really must. You can
          substitute with Stevia, but avoid aspartame.)
1/4   teaspoon turmeric
1   cup light rum or rum extract
         Nutmeg for garnish

Place everything but the soymilk into a blender. Turn on the blender, and when the mixture calms down, slowly pour in the soymilk until you've reached the consistency that pleases your gang. Serves 8.

Special note: If you make this a little thick, it makes a delightful creamy sauce you can use as a dessert topping. If you wish to omit the rum, that's okay; just increase the milk till desired consistency is achieved. Using the rum adds 410 additional calories per serving, if you're counting.

Pickled Ginger Dip

1   cup low-fat mayonnaise
1   cup nonfat sour cream
1   jar pickled ginger
1   tablespoon freshly chopped ginger
2   tablespoons chopped parsley

Remove half of the pickled ginger from the jar and squeeze with your hands. Reserve juice.

Combine all ingredients in a food processor and purée till smooth. Add salt and pepper to taste. If the mixture is too thick, add some of the reserved pickled ginger juice. Makes 2 $1/2$ cups.

Light Spinach Dip

If you must have a spinach dip, go for this healthier version.
(Recipe courtesy of Deb McClure-Smith)

6   tablespoons dehydrated minced or chopped onion
3   tablespoons unbleached all-purpose flour
1   tablespoon instant nonfat dry milk powder
$1/2$ teaspoon onion powder
$1/4$ teaspoon tumeric
$1/2$ teaspoon salt
2   10-ounce packages chopped frozen spinach, thawed
3   scallions, chopped
1   3-ounce can water chestnuts, chopped
$1 1/2$ cups low-fat sour cream
1   cup low-fat or nonfat mayonnaise

In a small bowl, combine onion, flour, milk powder, onion powder, turmeric, and salt.

Cook spinach in microwave for 5 minutes. Let cool and gently squeeze spinach to remove as much liquid as possible.

In a medium bowl, combine spinach, scallions, water chestnuts, sour cream, and mayonnaise. Add dry ingredients to spinach mixture and mix well. Chill several hours. Serve in a bowl or hollowed-out bread round.

Wheat-Free Chicken Nuggets

Occasionally, a complementary medicine practitioner will send a patient to my kitchen for some cooking advice for a child with allergies, most often to gluten. Gluten intolerance is quite common. After searching the Web, I ran across this recipe from McDonalds, made a few alterations, and bingo—the kids loved it! (As a matter of fact, the adults put a pretty good-size dent in the platter, too.)

Use any variety of dipping sauces, but beware of hidden sugar lurking below the surface. Be adventurous and make your own dipping sauces using sugar-free substitutes and nonfat bases, or try one of the sauces in this book. Sometimes you just have to be sneaky.

1	egg or ¼ cup liquid egg substitute
1	cup water
4	boneless, skinless chicken breast halves
½	cup amaranth flour
½	cup potato flour
2	tablespoons cornmeal
2	teaspoons sea salt
⅓	teaspoon black pepper
1	teaspoon onion powder
⅛	teaspoon garlic powder
1	teaspoon paprika
6	cups peanut oil

Beat the egg and the water together in a small, shallow bowl.

Combine flour, potato flour, corn meal, salt and pepper, onion and garlic powders, and paprika in a gallon-size plastic zipper bag.

Pound each chicken breast with a mallet until about ¼-inch thick. Cut each breast into bite-size pieces, and coat each piece with the flour mixture by shaking in the plastic bag gently—shake it, don't break it.

Remove and dredge each nugget in the egg mixture, coating well. Then return the nuggets to the flour mixture. Still with me? Shake again to coat, then arrange nuggets (don't stack them) on a sheet and freeze for at least one hour. Cover the remaining egg mix, and refrigerate both it and the coating mixture.

Preheat oven and a large cookie sheet to 375 degrees.

Remove nuggets from freezer and repeat the coating process.

In a deep-fat fryer (or heavy, deep saucepan), heat oil to 365 degrees. Be sure the oil is at the correct temperature: if it's too cool the nuggets will become oil-logged; if it's too hot, the nuggets will burn on the outside before they are done on the inside. Cook the nuggets till they're lightly golden and bob to the top.

Remove nuggets with a slotted spoon and drain on several layers of paper towels. Place nuggets on the preheated cookie sheet in the oven and bake for another 5–7 minutes—don't let 'em burn!

Serve with your favorite dipping sauce.

Pumpkin Spread

Caramelized onions impart a delightful flavor to this versatile mixture. Pumpkins are brimming with beta-carotene and fiber and are a first-line defense against heart disease.

2   tablespoons olive oil
4   medium yellow onions, sliced onionskin thin
1   regular size can of cooked pumpkin, drained (*not* pumpkin pie
        filling, however)
     Sea salt and black pepper
2   tablespoons real maple syrup

In a nonstick pan, sauté the onions in the olive oil over medium heat for at least fifteen minutes, stirring frequently with a wooden spoon every few minutes. Cook until the onions are caramelized. (Note: Caramelizing is the slow, but rewarding process of simmering the onions in their own natural sugars until they turn a dark brown.)

When the onions are caramelized, place them and the pumpkin in a food processor and blend to a smooth consistency. Add syrup and salt and pepper to taste.

Serving suggestions: Serve as a side entrée for any meal, a dip for crudités, a spread for crostini, or as a condiment for chicken or pork.

Sun-Dried Tomato and Bean Spread

Perfect for dipping with whole-wheat crackers or toasted slices of crostini.

$1/3$ cup chopped fresh basil
  3   ounces sun-dried tomatoes
  2   tablespoons tomato paste
  2   tablespoons balsamic vinegar
  1   tablespoon extra virgin olive oil
  1   tablespoon chopped scallions
$1/8$ teaspoon sea salt
$1/8$ teaspoon black pepper
  2   cloves minced garlic
  1   15-ounce can white beans, drained and rinsed
       Fat-free pita chips

Rehydrate the tomatoes in saucepan of simmering Marsala wine. (If you're really feeling bold, rehydrate the tomatoes in a good, stout port wine.) Combine the tomatoes with the remaining ingredients in a food processor and process until smooth.

☙

Two-Way Thai Summer Rolls

2   ounces bean thread noodles

2   tablespoons rice vinegar

2   carrots, peeled and julienned

12 ounces organic extra-firm silken tofu, julienned, or 8 ounces
      thinly slivered strips of lean pork loin or chicken breast

2   scallions, smashed and chopped

1/2 cup each chopped fresh mint, cilantro, and basil

2   minced garlic cloves

1   teaspoon freshly grated ginger

1   teaspoon fish sauce

2   tablespoons low-sodium soy sauce or shoyu

2   tablespoons fresh lime juice

1   tablespoon chile-garlic paste
    Sea salt

8   round rice paper sheets

1   tablespoon Spicy Hoisin Sauce (page 145)

1/2 cup coarsely chopped toasted peanuts
    Radicchio leaves

Have ready a large mixing bowl; one dry dish towel and one damp dish towel; a pot of water simmering on the stove; and an attractive serving platter.

Cover the noodles with boiling water and allow them to soak for about fifteen minutes. Drain, then toss the noodles with the vinegar and salt and set aside.

Blanch the carrots in boiling water for 2 minutes and drain.

Combine the carrots, tofu or meat, scallions, herbs, garlic, ginger, fish and soy sauce or shoyu, lime juice, and chile-garlic paste. Add salt to taste, and fold in the noodles.

Fill the large mixing bowl with very warm water, and soak the rice paper sheets until they become pliable, about 1 minute. Place the wet rice paper sheet on the flattened damp towel. Dab with the dry towel to remove excess water.

Place equal amounts of the filling on the bottom third of each rice sheet. Roll up the wraps egg-roll style: Grab the middle of each side and fold them in. Now grab the bottom and roll up to the top.

Line a serving platter with radicchio leaves and arrange the finished rolls on the platter. Garnish with toasted sesame seeds and a drizzle of Spicy Hoisin Sauce. Serve rolls cold or at room temperature.

Sweet Potato Fritters

(Or I Yam what I Yam!)

2	cups mashed sweet potatoes
1	tablespoon Sucanat
2	tablespoons real maple syrup
1	cup of low-fat skim milk or plain soymilk
4	tablespoons vegetable oil
2	eggs (separate the whites from the yolks, folks)
1/2	cup cooked quinoa
1/2	cup unbleached all-purpose flour
1	teaspoon aluminum-free baking powder
1/2	teaspooon sea salt

Cream the sweet potatoes with the Sucanat, maple syrup, milk, oil, and egg yolks. Add the quinoa and mix well.

Sift the flour, baking powder, and salt, and add to the sweet potato mixture.

Beat the egg whites mercilessly until stiff peaks form and fold into the batter. Do not overmix.

Heat a nonstick sauté pan over medium heat. Add 1/4 inch of vegetable oil for frying.

When heat reaches 365 degrees (use a thermometer for best results), place generous tablespoonfuls of the sweet potato mixture into the skillet. They should begin to sizzle immediately. With the back of the spoon, gently shape the fritters into round or oval shapes. Be neat.

Fry in batches until browned. Turn them only once! Adjust heat as needed so the fritters don't burn. Remove with a slotted spoon or spatula and place them on a doubled paper towel to drain.

This protein- and fiber-rich dish makes a great hors d'oeuvre or starch to round off a balanced dinner. Top the fritters with cinnamon flavored, nonfat sour cream or organic unsweetened applesauce.

Vegan Tapenade

½   cup pitted black olives
½   cup white beans, rinsed and drained
2   teaspoons capers
1   tablespoon chopped fresh garlic
¼   cup minced roasted red pepper
1   tablespoon coarsely ground black pepper
¼   cup chopped fresh parsley
4   teaspoons chopped onion
2   tablespoons fresh lemon juice
2   chopped scallions
2   teaspoons olive oil

Blend all ingredients in a food processor and spread on crusting rounds, tempeh, or chicken. You can also use it as a pizza topping or part of a Spanish tapas.

Barbeque Tempeh—Four Ways

1   package of multi-grain organic tempeh
2   teaspoons extra virgin olive oil
    Sea salt and pepper
RECOMMENDED SAUCES:
    Your favorite American barbeque sauce
    Spicy Hoisin Sauce (page 145)
    Sweet and Pungent Sauce (page 144)
    Cajun Spice Rub (page 147)

Cut tempeh into half-inch cubes. Warm the olive oil in a nonstick skillet over medium-high heat. Add the tempeh and sauté until lightly browned, about 10 minutes. Add salt and pepper to taste.

Toss the sautéed tempeh with one of the above sauces and bake in a 350 degree oven for 15 minutes to glaze on the 'cue. You can glaze on the barbecue in a skillet on the stovetop, but stay with it and don't walk away. You need to toss and turn them frequently or the sugars in the sauces will burn.

Special note: These meaty morsels can be used as a hors d'oeuvre or snacks for the kids. When you slice the cakes horizontally, they make great sandwiches. Cutting the tempeh into strips before you cook it will allow you to make a tempeh caesar salad, Cobb salad, or your everyday chef's salad.

Chili Nuts

4	cups of walnut pieces
2	tablespoons Sucanat
4	tablespoons Worcestershire sauce
2	tablespoons chili powder
1/2	teaspoon onion salt
1/2	teaspoon crushed red pepper

Combine all ingredients, except the nuts, in a saucepan and cook over low heat, stirring constantly.

Place the nuts into a large, round-sided mixing bowl. Add the warm seasoning mixture and toss to coat. (The aroma will drive you insane!)

Line a baking sheet with waxed paper and spray with nonstick spray. Spread the nuts evenly across the pan, making sure not to leave clumps. Bake at 350 degrees for 12–15 minutes or until toasted. Let cool and dive in.

Special note: Store in an airtight container. This full-bodied snack goes well with cocktails and makes a nutritious snack for the kids, too.

Curry Dip

This colorful concoction makes a wonderful dip for raw vegetables, a sauce for fish or chicken—or just eat it by the spoonful when no one's looking.

2	cups nonfat sour cream
6	ounces softened nonfat cream cheese
4	scallions, chopped
½	bunch fresh mint, minced
½	bunch fresh basil, minced
1	tablespoon tomato paste
1	teaspoon curry powder
1	teaspoon celery seed
2	tablespoons honey
2	tablespoons lemon juice
	Sea salt and pepper to taste

Combine all ingredients and mix well. Chill overnight for the best flavor.

CHAPTER THREE

Soups and Beverages

Since early times, after man was "primordial soup" himself, soups have been the nutritious staple of life. The Bible describes the "seething of pottage"(stew or soup) and early epics like *The Odyssey* show "B.C." villagers in ancient Greece putting vegetables and meat, and nuts and roots into pots to serve a whole crowd.

Soup is still wonderful nutrition. You can eat right with soup without ever opening a can.

And don't think meat is necessary to create tasty soup! You can create delicious vegetable broth with onions, herbs, tomatoes, squash, or a combination of vegetables. But good broth starts with the most important ingredient of all: good, clean water.

I'm going to spend a significant amount of time in this chapter talking about water, because water is at the very heart of good health, to say nothing of its importance as a basic cooking element, especially in soups and beverages. We need to care about water quality. Water from the tap—usually *yuck*. So I say this: you can either buy a filter or be a filter.

When I'm speaking, I sometimes ask audiences, "What do Jack and Jill who went up the hill have in common with explorer Ponce de Leon?"

Answer: They never took water for granted.

Ponce de Leon was on to something when he followed up on the rumors of an exotic island called Bimini, located somewhere north of Cuba, which was said to possess a crystal-clear bubbling spring with waters that had the power of restoring youth. He received a commission to try to find this wonderful water source, but obviously died anyway, so I guess he didn't find it. But, that's water under the bridge. At least you can say they were trying to find perfect water.

Did you know waterlogged Americans guzzled down over 5 billion gallons of bottled water in 2000?

The earth is composed of two-thirds water. We live on a watery planet, yet so few of us drink from that "fountain of youth." Like Planet Earth, our bodies are also two-thirds water, which is essential in every function of our earth suit. Water helps transport nutrients and waste products in and out of cells and is necessary for all digestive, absorptive, circulatory, and excretory functions, as well as for the utilization of water-soluble vitamins.

It has been said that a person can live about one month without food, but only about a week without water. Do you drink enough water, or do you find it unpalatable because it lacks sugar, carbonation, caffeine, or it just isn't hip? Most people believe they drink enough water, but a majority of physicians will admit most of us go around in a mild state of dehydration because we forget to drink the proper types and amounts of liquids.

You've heard this a hundred times if you've heard it once, "How am I going to get that much water down?" It's only sixty-four ounces folks, or eight 8-ounce glasses. It's not that tough if you don't mind sprinting to the bathroom more than usual, but you might want to cut back before going to bed. A glass first thing in the morning will help flush the toxins out of your body and rehydrate you from your eight-hour fast.

In our dreams we travel through pine forests and drink from pure streams of crystalline waters. In your dreams, folks. According to the EPA's Office of Water, States, Tribes, Territories, and Interstate Commissions Report in 1998, about 40 percent of U.S. streams, lakes, and estuaries that were assessed were not clean enough to support uses such as fishing and swimming. In 32 percent of all American waters tested, leading pollutants in impaired waters include siltation, bacteria, nutrients, and metals. Runoff from agricultural lands and urban areas is the primary source of these pollutants. Much remains to be done to restore and protect the nation's waters.

Over the last twenty years our water supply has been made an indiscriminate dumping ground, overwhelmed with chemicals and often deemed disastrous to our health. These cherished bodies of water are most often polluted from human industry, agricultural chemical and mining runoff, PCBs, septic tank seepage, oil wells, and toxic refuse sites. One of the most disgusting sources of water pollution comes from the animal waste produced by the brutally inhumane conditions which exist at all factory farms.

Forget trying to get water equivalencies through products other than H_2O. No doubt, as you shop, you curiously glance around at the other shoppers and assess their eating habits, noticing grocery carts brimming with cases of diet colas infused with caffeine and sweetened with aspartame, sugar-based fruit juices with artificial colorings, alcohol, homogenized milk, sports drinks, and the ineffective "functional" foods like ginseng cola, gota cola, chippy whippies, and echinacea fruit drinks. Most educated authorities will admit these drinks are useless and just a way to separate the consumer from his or her cash. With the way things are going, someday we'll probably be encouraged to drink Orwellian-style Prozac-infused water.

If you read the label on most of the sports drinks, you'll find at least three forms of sugar within the first five ingredients. The most popular diet meal-substitute drink lists sugar as its first ingredient. The calories provided by consuming sugar are calories empty of nutrition, as a result of overprocessing and manufacturing.

According to *The New York Times Guide to Personal Health*, "Drinks containing concentrated nutrients such as milk, sugar-sweetened soft drinks, and salty tomato-based juices, count more as food than drink since they themselves increase your body's water needs."

Could good, clean, fresh water actually be the fountain of youth? It may well be. Still—does drinking water turn you off? Slosh these facts around.

- We tend to take water for granted. Only those deprived of it fully realize its value.
- There is the same amount of water on earth as there was when the earth was formed. The water from your faucet could contain molecules that dinosaurs drank.
- Most foods contain plenty of water. You obtain $3^{1}/_{2}$ cups from what is eaten over the course of a day, providing you eat plenty of fruits and vegetables.
- Water suppresses the appetite and helps the body metabolize stored fat. An increase in water consumption can actually help to reduce fat deposits.
- Water helps maintain proper muscle tone by giving your muscles their natural ability to contract and by preventing dehydration.
- To judge how much fluid you lose during a sweaty aerobic workout, weigh yourself before and after you exercise.
- When exercising, drink two cups of fluid for every pound of body weight lost. Most people's thirst will be satisfied after consuming only about two-thirds of the fluid lost. But don't stop there.
- Water regulates the earth's temperature. It also regulates the temperature of the human body, carries nutrients and oxygen to cells, cushions joints, protects organs and tissues, and removes wastes. It can also help relieve constipation.
- Seventy-five percent of the human brain is water and 75 percent of a living tree is water. And, 70 percent of your skin is water.
- Carbonated water may cause stomach and intestinal distress, and thus may result in a decrease in the amount of fluid you consume.

If you have any suspicions regarding the quality of your water, the *Environmental Nutrition Newsletter* suggests three courses of action:

- Check your yearly local water quality report and note violations.

- Have your own water tested straight from the tap. Contact your local health department for the names and numbers of certified labs.
- If your tap water is not safe or palatable, use a home filter or filtering pitcher.

Whether you plan to drink or cook with water, it's always best to opt for the filtered versions to protect your family from risks.

Water is most of all cleansing to the system. After an eating splurge, you may wish to consider fasting for a day to let the water you take in purge your system of unwholesome substances.

Over twenty-four hundred years ago, our mentor Hippocrates, the father of medicine, used fasting to combat disease and clean out the system.

Fasting is a cost-effective therapy for a constellation of human maladies including hypertension, headaches, allergies, and arthritis. Of course, it is prudent to consult your family physician before you attempt a fast, and then keep him informed of what you are doing.

To prepare for a fast, eat only raw vegetables and fruits for two days. This will make the fast less of a shock to the system. The desired effects of the fast can be ruined by eating cooked foods immediately afterward. Because the stomach and the amount of secreted digestive juices may decrease during fasting, the first meals after a fast should be frequent and small. If you must eat something during the fast, eat a piece of watermelon, or fresh, not canned, applesauce. Make the applesauce in a blender and leave the skins on. Do not cook the apples.

The following fasting recipes are from Kripalu Center for Yoga and Health in Lennox, Massachusetts. They are based on the use of juices to keep the body from dehydrating and to give basic energy.

I need to add a warning on Spirulina. Although its healthful attributes are well-documented, it does contain large amounts of vitamin K. If you are a heart patient taking coumadin and you wish to fast, consult your doctor. Vitamin K encourages formation of blood clots.

Fasting for a Day

These drinks for fasting are also excellent beverages when used in a normal day to achieve the proper levels of water consumption.

THE REGIMEN:

(Note: The recipes for the fasting beverages are on pages 40–41.)

When you wake up—1 cup (8 ounces) of Lemon Spring Water (warm or cold), then,
10 A.M.—8 to 10 ounces of Apple-Cranberry Juice
12:30 P.M.—8 to 10 ounces of Carrot-Ginger Juice
3 P.M.—8 to 10 ounces of Apple-Cucumber Juice
5:30 P.M.—2 cups (16 ounces) of Vegetable Broth

Throughout the day, drink Lemon Spring Water

But now, using all the fresh water you've found, and aware of its many benefits, let's get into the specific food preparation recipes for soups and beverages that you'll now be enjoying.

Eat Right Recipes

FASTING BEVERAGES

Lemon Spring Water

2   quarts spring water
     Juice of two organic lemons
¼   teaspoon Stevia (optional)

Place water in a pitcher. Stir in lemon juice, add Stevia to sweeten to taste.

Apple-Cranberry Juice

1   large apple, cut up (everything but the stem)
¼   cup cranberries

Place ingredients into a juicer and process.

Carrot-Ginger Juice

3   large organic carrots, cut up
½   teaspoon minced or grated fresh ginger

Place ingredients into a juicer and process.

Apple-Cucumber Juice

¼   green apple (including skin and seeds)
1   organic cucumber, cut up
1   handful of washed parsley

Place ingredients into a juicer and process.

Vegetable Broth

3 cups water
1 large potato
1/2 cup each of carrots, celery, grated beets, and sliced onion
2 cloves of garlic
1 bay leaf
   Pinch each of thyme and cayenne pepper

Place all the ingredients in a nonreactive pot and bring to a boil. Lower heat and simmer for one hour. Strain vegetables from broth and discard.

MORE BEVERAGES

Watermelon Spritzer

2 cups cold watermelon
3 tablespoons orange juice concentrate
1 tablespoon honey, Sucanat, or Stevia powder
1 tablespoon lime juice
2 cups soda water
1 tablespoon maple syrup
4 to 5 ounces light rum (or several drops of rum extract)

Place all ingredients in a blender and let 'er rip. If you want it colder, add a crushed ice cube or two during the blending process. Garnish with additional watermelon wedges. Serves 6.

Raja's Cup Latté

If you're one of those trying to wean yourself off coffee because of the four hundred or so approved chemicals used in its production, then you might want to consider this delicious beverage. Raja's Cup is the nutrionally desirable antioxidant coffee substitute, and it's one-hundred-percent caffeine-free to boot. You can purchase it at a nutrition-conscious food store.

Boil some filtered water and make the Raja's Cup per package instructions. Add a dash of Stevia and a pinch of cinnamon. Mix the Raja's Cup half-and-half with room-temperature vanilla soymilk.

SOUPS

Fidel's Cuban Black Bean Soup

1	tablespoon extra virgin olive oil
1	cup yellow chopped onion
1	finely minced jalapeño pepper (protect hands with plastic food-service gloves or plastic wrap when working with peppers)
½	teaspoon dried oregano
½	teaspoon dried thyme
12	ounces diced ham (or use liquid smoke to taste)
2	powdered bay leaves
1	crushed red pepper
	Sea salt
4	cups black beans, cooked, rinsed, and drained
⅓	cup dark rum
1	cup nonfat sour cream

Place a large pot on the stove over medium heat and add the olive oil. When oil is hot, add the onions and cook until they are tender. (Love me tender, Momma.)

Now stir in the jalapeño pepper, oregano, thyme, ham or liquid smoke, bay leaf, and crushed red pepper. Add salt to taste.

Add the black beans and rum. Continue cooking over medium heat, stirring frequently, 8–10 minutes, or till heated through.

Remove about 1 cup of the bean mixture, place it in a mixing bowl, and mash it either with a fork or a potato masher. You can also use a food processor or blender. Add the mashed beans back into the soup. Continue to simmer over low heat, stirring so the bottom will not scorch. Serves 4.

Serving suggestion: Top with sour cream over a bed of grain and serve with a large garden salad and some whole-wheat bread. If you wish, add some small pieces of chicken.

Five-a-Day Soup

This nourishing soup is almost too simple. Make a large batch and freeze some for future use. You'll be glad you did.

$1/2$ cup of each of the following: finely chopped onion, mushrooms, carrot, sweet potato, celery, green pepper, and an apple (with skin)
4   cups vegetable stock or defatted chicken stock
$1/2$ head cabbage, thinly shaved
1   pound of spinach leaves, stemmed
1   bay leaf
4   cloves fresh garlic, minced
1   10-ounce can of diced tomatoes in juice
    Sea salt and pepper to taste
    Chopped fresh parsley

Combine all ingredients, except the parsley, in a large nonreactive pot. (The reason I suggest using a nonreactive pot is that aluminum, cast iron, or copper pots leach their metal into the food, altering the content and often the appearance of the dish. Absorbing too many heavy metals can also damage your precious health.)

Bring just to a boil, then reduce heat to medium and simmer for 15 minutes. Toss in the parsley just before serving.

Special note: This nourishing soup is better the second day. Ladle some over a bowl half-filled with warm grains. Add chicken or beans to increase the protein content. Add pastas, but don't put it in until you are ready to serve, so the pasta won't get overcooked and gummy.

Minestrone

When cooking soups, always opt for preparing a large batch, some for immediate consumption and the rest for freezer.

4	ounces olive oil
2	large onions, chopped
1	entire stalk of celery, chopped
1	pound of carrots, chopped
1	pound of shredded white cabbage
1	3-pound can of tomatoes, with juice
8	cloves of minced fresh garlic
2	cups dry red wine
1½	gallons vegetable or chicken stock
2	bay leaves, powdered
2	tablespoons dried thyme
1	can garbanzo beans, drained and rinsed
1	can kidney beans, drained and rinsed
1	pound of cooked whole-grain elbow macaroni pasta
	Sea salt and pepper
1	bunch scallions, finely chopped
1	tablespoon Parmesan cheese per person, for garnish

Pull out your largest stockpot and place it over a medium fire, then add the olive oil, garlic, cabbage, carrots, celery, chopped onions, bay, and thyme. Sauté and stir for two minutes.

Add the canned tomatoes, wine, and stock. Cook until the vegetables are tender, perhaps 10 minutes. Stir up from the bottom to prevent scorching.

Add the beans and pasta and cook just till pasta is done—not too long or the pasta will turn mushy. Always add the pasta at the end of cooking. Add salt and pepper to taste. Sprinkle with scallions and Parmesan cheese and serve. Makes 2 gallons.

∾

Cream of Mushroom Soup

4 tablespoons extra virgin olive oil
3/4 cup finely minced white onion
1 teaspoon fresh thyme leaves
   Scant pinch of ground nutmeg
1/3 cup sherry
1 pound white, cultivated mushrooms, thinly sliced
1 pound shiitake mushrooms, stems removed, and thinly sliced
3 1/2 cups low-sodium, low-fat chicken stock
1/2 cup reconstituted nonfat dry milk, made extra strong
1/2 cup nonfat sour cream

Grab a large pot, place it over medium heat. Add the oil, and when it is hot, add the onion, thyme, and nutmeg. (Nutmeg can be overpowering, so be careful not to overdo it.) Sauté for 2 minutes.

Add the sherry and cook till it has slightly reduced. Add the mushrooms and continue to sauté for 5 minutes, stirring frequently. Add the stock, milk, and the sour cream.

Now it is time for you to decide if the soup needs to be thicker. If so, compose a cornstarch slurry of a little cornstarch mixed with water. Bring the soup to a boil and add the cornstarch slurry, a little at a time, until you've reached the desired consistency. Stir, stir, stir! Serves 4.

Oriental Noodle and Cabbage Soup

3 pounds white or Napa cabbage, thinly sliced
1 tablespoon peanut oil
8 cloves of finely minced garlic
1 teaspoon freshly grated ginger
1 jalapeño pepper, minced (protect hands with plastic food-service
     gloves or plastic wrap when working with hot peppers)
12 fresh shiitake mushrooms
6 cups defatted chicken or vegetable stock
1/4 cup Chinese rice wine or sake
2 ounces of either rice or soba noodles, cooked
   Sea salt and pepper

In a large pot, heat the oil over medium heat, then add the garlic, ginger, hot pepper, and mushrooms. Stir-fry for about 30 seconds.

Now, add 1 cup of chicken broth and the rice wine or sake, and then cover. Simmer for about 5 or 6 minutes.

Carefully lift off the lid and add the remainder of the broth. Bring to a boil, then reduce the heat to low and simmer uncovered for 30 minutes.

Add the cabbage and noodles. Cook, constantly stirring, for 2 minutes, or until the cabbage wilts. Add salt and pepper to taste. Serves 6.

Red Lentil and Barley Stew

(Recipe courtesy of Deb McClure-Smith)

1	large onion, diced
4	cloves garlic, minced
1	teaspoon oregano
2	teaspoons curry powder
$1/2$	teaspoon dried thyme
$1/4$	teaspoon black pepper
2	bay leaves
$1/4$	cup red wine
2	medium sweet potatoes, peeled and diced
2	stalks celery, diced
$2/3$	cup pearled barley
$2^{1/4}$	cup red lentils, rinsed and sorted
1	28-ounce can crushed tomatoes
$1/4$	cup tamari or Bragg Liquid Aminos*
1	tablespoon orange juice concentrate

Spray a large pot with nonstick spray; add onion, garlic, oregano, curry powder, thyme, and pepper. Sauté, stirring constantly over medium heat. Add bay leaves and wine and continue cooking until onion is tender, about 5 minutes.

Add 2 cups water and stir in sweet potatoes, celery, and barley. Continue to cook 5 minutes, stirring to prevent sticking.

Add lentils, tomatoes and 7 more cups of water, and tamari or Liquid Aminos. Bring to a boil. Cover and turn to low. Simmer 45 minutes or until lentils and barley are tender. Add orange juice near the end of cooking. Remove bay leaves and serve.

    * *Found in most whole food stores.*

Pumpkin Soup

3	tablespoons olive oil
1	medium onion, chopped
1	cup of a mixture of chopped red, green, and yellow peppers
1/8	teaspoon crushed red pepper (optional)
1	teaspoon cinnamon
1	teaspoon curry powder
1	teaspoon cumin
1/2	teaspoon coriander
1	teaspoon minced fresh ginger
1/2	teaspoon minced garlic
1	cup Madeira wine (and a sip for you)
6	cups pumpkin purée
2	cups vegetable stock or, if you wish, defatted chicken stock
1	cup water
2	cups skim milk or plain soymilk
	Sea salt
	Plain organic yogurt
	Chopped cilantro

In a large pot, over medium-high heat, add the oil, then the onions, peppers, crushed red pepper (if desired), cinnamon, curry, cumin, coriander, ginger, and garlic. Stir and cook for 2 minutes.

Now add the wine and the pumpkin purée and warm them until they get to know each other. Add the stock and water and bring the mixture to a boil. Reduce heat to medium and simmer, stirring constantly, for about 15 minutes.

All right, the hard part's over. Pull out your food processor or blender, and purée the soup, in small batches, till smooth. Heat expands, so be cautious just in case the top of the blender pops off. Ouch!

Return the hot mix to the pot and add the skim or soy milk. Add salt to taste, and adjust other seasonings to your preference. Garnish with a tablespoon of plain yogurt and a dusting of chopped cilantro leaves. Serves 8 to 10.

Miso Shiitake Soup

5	cups water
1	strip of kombu*
1	teaspoon fresh, minced ginger
2	cloves of minced garlic
2	tablespoons dry sherry (not cooking sherry)
1/2	cup carrots, small dice
1	cup washed, stemmed, and thinly julienned fresh shiitake mushrooms
1	cup snow peas, washed and de-stringed
3	tablespoons white miso paste

Place the water, kombu, ginger, garlic, sherry, carrots, and mushrooms in a pot. Bring it to a boil and simmer for 10 minutes. Remove the kombu, slice it very, very thin, and add it back to the stock.

Reduce heat to low and add the miso and snow peas. Simmer for 1 minute. Serve.

*A type of dried seaweed found in Asian markets or the Asian food section of most grocery stores.

Southwestern Bean Stew

2	teaspoons extra virgin olive oil
2	jalapeño peppers, seeded and chopped (protect hands with plastic food-service gloves or plastic wrap when working with hot peppers)
1	medium onion, minced

2   cups of a mixture of diced red, green, and yellow peppers
1   tablespoon minced fresh garlic
1   tablespoon chili powder
1   tablespoon cocoa powder
6   cloves minced fresh garlic
2   cups chopped tomatoes, with juice
¼   cup dry sherry
2   pounds beans (preferably pinto), cooked, drained, and rinsed
2   tablespoons wheat germ
2   cups vegetable stock or chicken stock
2   tablespoons each of chopped cilantro, scallion, and parsley
    Nonfat sour cream

In a large stockpot, add the oil, and heat over medium fire. Add the jalapenos, onion, peppers, garlic, and chili and cocoa powders. Enjoy the aroma?

Now add the tomatoes, sherry, beans, stock, and wheat germ. Simmer for just 5 minutes, stirring gently, so as not to break up the beans. Just before serving, add the chopped parsley, cilantro, and scallions. Top with nonfat sour cream and serve. Olé, baby! Serves 10.

Special note: Serve over a bed of grain along with some tasty corn-bread. Add chicken, pork, or seafood for the meat eaters in the group.

Beano Spritzer

If the musical accompaniment provided when you consume beans is a concern, serve your guests this tasty cocktail before your next bean supper and there will be peace in the valley.

Combine some soda water and white wine with a dash of Beano and serve over ice, just as you would with any other spritzer. The only difference with this spritzer is that you're adding the gas-squelching qualities of Beano.

ᕽ

CHAPTER FOUR

Salads, Dressings, and Vegetable Dishes

It was a dark and stormy night with not a vegetable in sight. Not a green, leafy salad on a plate with light olive oil and garlic dressing. Had the salad army been there, they might have been able to combat the enemy: free radicals.

The joint was lousy with uncontrolled radicals on the loose, lurking at every corner, itchy for their next hit, relentlessly chipping away millions of times per day at the foundation of our health, our molecules. Is it too late, or can we defend our earth suits from these thugs? Since birth we've allowed these thugs to terrorize, to indiscriminately steal electrons from our molecules and oxidize them into submission.

These free radicals, which sound like the lovable, tree-hugging, granola-crunching peaceniks from the sixties, are here, there, and everywhere under the sun. Free radicals are parts of molecules that act at the cellular level to destroy health by oxidizing certain organic compounds in the human body. We are unable to go an entire day of eating, absorbing, inhaling, snorting, swallowing, smoking, drinking, or sunbathing without being exposed to these aggressive pathogens which repeatedly attack our healthy cells and cause them to lose their structure and function. Free radicals are caused by environmental toxic chemical exposure. A real drag. Just the other day, a rather large diesel dump truck engulfed my vehicle in a bluish-black cloud of smoke, and before I could get the window up, cough, gasp . . . the entire auto was filled with this carcinogenic diesel exhaust. Free radicals are very hard, if not impossible, to avoid.

Here is just a small sampling of the delightful conditions, diseases, and disorders that have been attributed to free radicals damage: atherosclerosis, age spots, cancer, multiple sclerosis, attention deficit disorder, cold feet, cold fingers, pulmonary dysfunction, cataracts, arthritis and inflammatory diseases, diabetes, shock, trauma, and ischemia, renal disease, strokes, migraine headaches, senility, kidney and liver damage, male sexual inadequacy, blindness, phlebitis, skin cancer, varicose veins, pancreatitis, inflammatory bowel disease and colitis, Parkinson's disease, neonatal lipoprotein oxidation, drug reactions, skin lesions, and premature aging. The list could go on and on.

Antioxidants are ammo to combat these frightening, roaming radicals. Antioxidants work in several ways: They may reduce the energy of the free radical, stop the free radical from forming in the first place, or interrupt an oxidizing chain reaction to minimize the damage of free radicals.

Antioxidants are found in several substances in foods. Specific ones are nutraceuticals, phytochemicals, phytonutrients, phytofoods, and functional foods. Who dreamed up this technology? They've been around a while, but what's new is that since the eighties, science has added the knowledge about the disease-preventing components they contain. Dr. Stephen de Felice, M.D., Director of New York's Foundation for Innovation in Medicine, is credited with the first use of the term nutraceutical, which describes specific chemical compounds found in foods that may prevent disease. It's all about good, free radical-fighting food.

Food can be good or bad, of course, in trying to combat the ills brought on us by free radicals. Food is grown in soil, dirt. Insects and molds live in the crops grown in the soil, and unenlightened farmers use pesticides to kill these insects. And it is from pesticide pollution that the free radical problem occurs.

Exhale deeply and inhale these facts: During the past decade, pesticide poisonings have increased 100 percent. In 1990, American manufacturers emitted more than 2.4 billion—that's with a "B"—

pounds of toxic pollutants into the atmosphere. The annual health cost of human exposure to outdoor air pollutants in the U.S. is nearly $50 billion. To find out about current environmental legislative proposals, go to www.epa.gov/epahome/rules.html#legislation.

Following is the USDA's list of the twelve most contaminated foods (in order of degree of contamination—note the tie on number 2):

1. Strawberries
2. Red and green bell peppers
2. Spinach (tied with the peppers)
3. North American cherries
4. Peaches
5. Mexican cantaloupe
6. Celery
7. Apples
8. Apricots
9. Green Beans
10. Chilean grapes
11. Cucumbers

I recommend that you purchase produce with fewer, toxic, health-compromising pesticides for the sake of your loved ones.

A diet rich in beautifully colored fruits and vegetables has the most benefit against aging and cancer caused in part by free radicals. Antioxidants, with all those hard to pronounce names, are present in colored fruits. Choose red instead of green grapes, red grapefruit instead of white, dark leafy green vegetables, broccoli, beets, green beans, and peas. Chow down some beta-carotene-rich, orange veggies such as sweet potatoes, carrots, and dark orange squashes. Of course, whenever possible, choose organic produce. Produce power! Fruit salads! Cool vegetable blends!

Specifically, terpenes are found in green foods, soy products, and grains, carotenoids found in orange, yellow, and red plant pigments such as those found in tomatoes, parsley, oranges, pink grapefruit, and spinach. All the elements of a fine summer salad: tomato slices, right from the garden, sprinkled with basil and snipped parsley. Or a winter plate, served as a luncheon entree: grapefruit and orange slices on spinach with a honey-olive oil dressing.

Phytoesterols occur in most green and yellow vegetables, and it is their seeds that contain the most concentrated sterols. Phyto-esterols have also been discovered in pumpkin seeds, sweet potatoes, soy, rice, and herbs. Many new salads with brown rice bases will fit the bill

EAT RIGHT AND LIVE LONGER

Researchers in Japan, who have been studying the health benefits of fruits and vegetables for thirty years, agree it is likely that a lifestyle that includes lots of colored fruits and vegetables is the key to health and longevity. Takeshi Hirayama, M.D., who led the study, concluded that the "speed of aging is likely to be controlled by lifestyle modification. Smoking cessation, avoiding or limiting alcohol and meat consumption and increased consumption of colored fruit and vegetables must be the wisest and healthiest way to live."

If you do your research and read the available literature, you will discover that science has proven that people who consume large amounts of beta-carotene from fruits and vegetables have a dramatically lower risk of lung cancer than those who consume less. More is better, in this instance.

Ironically, studies have indicated that there is some evidence that taking beta-carotene supplements (33,000 to 50,000 IU per day) can actually increase the risk of lung cancer by 18–20 percent. The same thing has been discovered about vitamin A. Downing whole handfuls of vitamins isn't a good idea. So don't overdo it—a good rule for all parts of healthful living. Your liver will thank you.

To reap a harvest of preventative benefits from phytonutrients, authorities suggest five to seven portions a day. A portion is simply ½ cup and it's easier than you imagine to achieve the daily portions. Fruit, juice, and grain cereal for breakfast, two ounces of clean and lean protein, green salad and grain bread at lunch, legumes, red wine, and veggies for supper, and you're all set.

But don't take the good benefits of salad greens and vegetables for granted. Not all vegetables are equal. The beautifully arranged produce in the grocery was packed in the growing field and whatever flew or walked over it and left a gift, is still there. In recent years, *E. coli* and salmonella have been discovered to have caused severe illness and death in children who consumed water-melon at a chain steak-house restaurant and coleslaw from one of America's favorite fried chicken places.

Wash your fruits and veggies as if your family's life depended on it. Hard running cold water and a little scrub brush can rid the produce of any deadly pathogens or fill a sink with cold water and add just a few drops of bleach, soak, rinse, and chomp.

The bottom line: Lower the rate of damage by decreasing your rate of exposure from free radical oxidants like pesticides, dry cleaning chemicals, alcohol, drugs, radiation, and smoking, and increase antioxidant protection as you grow older and, hopefully, a little bit wiser. Eating intelligently and taking your vitamins are your best defenses. Hey, forget what the neighbors think—go hug a tree and crunch some granola, since science proves it has never harmed anyone, except for, maybe, when naturalist Ewell Gibbons reportedly choked on a wild hickory nut.

But salads and vegetables are good for more than just combating free radicals. A diet based on salad greens and vegetables can also combat heart attacks. This green and colored vegetable-based diet should go a long way toward replacing the meat-based and overly fatty diet many Americans now consume, a diet that is ruining their hearts and shortening their lives.

exactly. Pumpkin seeds can go on many combination fruit and vegetable salads, and of course sprinkled herbs dress up greens so they are ready to go to the dance!

Our fourth group of antioxidant-rich phytonutrients is the widely studied phenols, which are found in blue, blue-red, and violet foods such as berries, grapes, and purple eggplant. Picture a perfect salad plate with seedless organic grapes, juicy blackberrries and strawberries and oranges, with pumpkin bread on the side.

Here we go with the lists of good foods and bad foods to combat free radicals and hold off heart attacks:

Good Foods

Organic fresh veggies, lots of fresh garlic, nuts, whole grains and brown rice, beans, tofu, and legumes, flax seed or oil, fiber, organic fruits and berries, a glass of red wine now and then, lots of water, pumpkin, whole-grain pasta, tempeh, salmon and other cold-water fish, and olive oil. Basically, this is the Mediterranean diet we touted in Chapter One.

Bad Foods

Sugar, dairy, junk food, fast food, deep-fried foods, solid fats (basically from all land animals), organ meats, trans-heated or partially hydrogenated oil or fats, white foods like flour and white rice. These white foods are linked with diabetes because of their rapid absorption and conversion to sugar, causing fast changes in sugar–insulin balance. They also lack nutrients. So, don't eat your heart out.

And finally, on the topic of dairy products, another white food, sip on this: We are the only species on the planet that drinks milk from another species. You ever see two dogs holding Fluffy the Cat down while Spot and Ruff take a good long drink? Picture, if you will, the two dogs with white mustaches saying, "Milk, it does a doggie good!"

Whatever action you decide to take, remember that an active lifestyle and proper nutrition is crucial for heart health, along with a good sense of humor. Laughter, smiles, and faith were my miracles. There is a miracle out there with your name on it.

And cut, cut, cut the fat!

Now, let's get down to brass tacks—err—grass snacks—and figure out how to fix sensational slimming salads that work to defeat the twin villains: free radicals and their companion general ill health and heart disease.

Everything revolves around the fork.

— Howard Lyman, author, *The Mad Cowboy*

DAD

My own personal experience confirms what too much fat—combined with other causes—may have done in our family. Salads were an important part of our meals when my brothers and I sat down at the table in the evening. A big bowl of iceberg or leaf lettuce, chopped celery, cucumbers, peppers (Mom called them mangos), doused with bottled or homemade dressing, and always a vegetable—these were a must in my mother's meal planning. But these could hardly have balanced the high-fat, country-style, meat-and-potatoes diet we all lived on.

Of course, back in those days, we lived to eat, rather than ate to live.

Unfortunately, we didn't know any better. I hesitantly recall my childhood when my brothers and I would fight over the delicious, crispy skin of Mom's moist and delicious fried chicken. In retrospect, that's actually rather gross: We actually fought over who would get the crispy skin of a dead barn foul.

Did you really know why the chicken crossed the road? To prove to the possum it could be done before both of them were chopped up with cream gravy for someone's high-fat dinner. That's my own variant of how the saying goes out in the country.

These high-fat foods could have contributed to the massive coronary which took my father at the age of forty-seven.

I was seventeen. I could hear the crunch of gravel as Dad's car pulled onto the driveway and into the garage, when, as usual, I flipped on the floodlight that illuminated the garage and our basketball court where my two older brothers and I would play well into the night with the neighborhood gang.

As Dad exited the car, I couldn't help but notice he was sweating from head to toe, soaked to the bone. Not a soul at home but me.

When he got inside the kitchen, I observed he was struggling to breathe, blue in the face, as he headed for the bedroom to change his clothes. The next noise I heard was a thud. Dad was gone from coronary artery disease before he hit the floor.

A jumbo blood clot became dislodged from one of his main arteries. Bingo. For the rest of my life I have not forgotten the deep blue color of Dad's face, the head to toe sweat, the thud, and finally my aunt coming upstairs to my bedroom holding me in her arms and telling me, "Your Daddy's gone." I was seventeen! At that time, CPR was unheard of, 911 was just three numbers, aspirin was for pain, and when it came to symptoms of a heart attack, we were clueless.

As my brothers and I each approached our own forty-seventh birthdays, we wondered what had brought on Dad's fatal heart condition. Then it dawned on us that Dad worked thirty years for Texaco in a nonfiltered, smoke-filled office. Dad would come home each evening reeking of smoke. No one knew then, of course, how deadly secondhand smoke could be. So, we figured that, along with the overly rich fat-based diet we consumed, must have killed my father.

Moral: We must all be aware of the connection of high-fat, low vegetable, bad-lifestyle diets and heart disease.

NUTRITION AND LIFESTYLE —
SOME FOLKS JUST DON'T GET IT!

Denial is not a luxury reserved for the naive and the young, as I discovered this one morning while waiting in my cardiologist's waiting room. A rather obese gentleman in his sixties, waiting while his wife was seen by the doctor, bragged about his diabetes and obesity to any who would listen. He proclaimed that eating overly rich, fatty foods had not caused him any health problems! He also admitted to hard drinking all his life and "It didn't do me no harm."

I began to boil. He began berating people who were appearing on the waiting room TV screen, sharing their inspiring weight-loss stories with happy endings. The obviously unhappy gentleman was ridiculing them: "How'd y'all get that fat to begin with?" Okay, that was it for me! My blood pressure and heart rate began to rise and I could hold my tongue no longer.

"You look overweight yourself, why are you so critical of them?" I asked. "Are you a religious man?"

"Oh, yup, sure am."

"Do you believe that your earth suit is a gift from God to house your soul throughout your earthly life?"

"Yes, definitely," he answered, with a look that said, *Okay, where are you going with this?*

"Then why do you heap contempt upon your creator by abusing yourself?" The room went quiet as the other patients in the room hung onto my words and waited for his reaction.

I inquired whether he had diabetes: Yes. Do you have heart disease: Yes. Are you overweight? Yeah. Is a physician treating you? "No, and damn proud of it. Doesn't bother me, so why should I care?"

As Bob Dylan said, we usually criticize or make fun of what we don't understand, comprehend, or can't conquer.

HEART ATTACKS IN AMERICA

According to 1998 statistics, 60,800,000 Americans have one or more forms of cardiovascular disease:

High blood pressure 50,000,000
Coronary heart disease 12,400,000
Myocardial infarction (acute heart attack) 7,300,000
Angina pectoris (chest pain) 6,400,000
Stroke 4,500,000
Rheumatic fever/rheumatic heart disease 1,800,000

Source: American Heart Association

These are mind-blowing statistics considering the fact that the disease is largely preventable.

The American Heart Association lists the six primary risk factors that must be corrected for the prevention of cardiovascular disease. They are also risk factors for some cancers, and include

- Obesity
- High blood cholesterol
- High blood pressure
- Diabetes mellitus
- Cigarettes and tobacco smoke
- Lack of physical activity

Weight loss removes some of the risk of heart disease. Exercise helps tremendously. It's your body: use it or lose it.

What exactly is coronary heart disease? Well, it is caused by atherosclerotic narrowing of the coronary arteries, which is likely to produce angina pectoris, heart attack, or both. Plaque build-up can cause a blockage or a blood clot.

Heart attack warning signals include chest pain or discomfort; arm pain or numbness; shortness of breath; profuse sweating; nausea, vomiting; dizziness, lightheadedness; weakness, fatigue, malaise; jaw or neck pain; heart palpitations; back pain; sense of impending doom. (Source: *Archives of Internal Medicine*)

In a heart attack emergency, do not waste precious minutes weighing your options. Act immediately.

- Call 911. Calling your own doctor may waste valuable time.
- Describe the symptoms such as severe shortness of breath or chest pain. This ensures a priority dispatch of EMS responders trained in basic and advanced cardiac life support
- Begin CPR. If you are not trained, a dispatcher can instruct you in CPR until help arrives.
- Decide on the fastest method of transportation. Ideally, responders should reach you within five minutes. However, if you live within four to five minutes of a hospital you might get there quicker.
- Pop an aspirin and chew it up. Aspirin inhibits blood clotting, which helps maintain blood flow through a narrow artery. This simple act can decrease death rates by about 25 percent.

But the point I really want to make is that, more than anything else, the food you eat and the lifestyle you lead can prevent heart attacks.

A dear friend works as a nutritionist in the cardiovascular rehabilitation program for a major Indianapolis hospital. She tells jaw-dropping stories of post-cardiac surgery patients arriving for counseling and rehab, toting with them bags of fast-food burgers and fries, cookies, and candy. They just don't realize that they're just one chicken nugget away from another heart attack.

You can still heap your plate! But instead of heaping it with red meats and heavy, fattening foods, fill it up with salads and vegetables!

Eat Right Recipes

SALADS AND VEGETABLE DISHES

Tuscan White Bean Salad

1   package fresh oregano, washed and patted dry
1   15-ounce can cannellini beans, drained and rinsed
1   small can of artichoke pieces (not in oil)
2   scallions, minced
    Extra virgin olive oil
    Kosher or sea salt and black pepper to taste
1   tablespoon minced garlic
1   tablespoon lemon juice
1   teaspoon vitamin C crystals
    Freshly grated Asiago cheese

Remove the leaves from the oregano stems and mince lightly. Reserve a little for the final garnish.

Drain and rinse the beans and the artichokes. In a mixing bowl, combine all ingredients, except the cheese, and mix. Add as much or as little olive oil as you wish. Note: In this dish, extra virgin olive oil is one of the main flavors, so don't use cheap olive oil or you'll be disappointed.

Allow the finished dish to rest for a while so the flavors can marry. Garnish with reserved oregano and serve at room temperature. Serves 4.

Sweet Potato Salad
with Maple Mustard Dressing

$^1/_2$ cup vegetable oil
2   tablespoons cider vinegar
2   tablespoons real maple syrup
2   tablespoons organic wheat germ
2   tablespoons Dijon mustard
$^1/_4$ teaspoon dry mustard
2   tablespoons dried thyme (or 4 tablespoons fresh thyme)
3   pounds sweet potatoes
    Sea salt and black pepper

In a small bowl, whisk together the oil, vinegar, syrup, wheat germ, Dijon and dry mustards, and thyme. Refrigerate.

Preheat oven to 375 degrees. Thoroughly wash the sweet potatoes and cut into 1-inch cubes. Do not peel! Place the sweet potatoes on a baking sheet pan and spray with nonstick spray to coat. Salt and pepper to taste. Roast the potatoes for 25 minutes or until tender. (Squeeze a piece between two fingers, and if it is soft, they're ready.)

While the potatoes are still warm, gently toss them with the dressing. Don't overtoss or they'll turn to mush. For best flavor, serve at room temperature. Serves 8.

Caribbean Cobb Salad

A California-based salad converted to the island of St. Croix, this dish relies on the fruity mango for its richness.

5   tablespoons extra virgin olive oil
2   tablespoons red wine vinegar
2   teaspoons habañero hot pepper sauce
$^1/_2$ teaspoon sea salt
    Freshly cracked black pepper
1   tablespoon chopped fresh thyme
1   pound large shrimp, peeled, deveined, and cooked

2   large, firm mangos, peeled and diced
1   cucumber (run a fork down the sides and slice into pretty half-moons)
1   avocado, peeled, and sliced into six wedges
1/2   red pepper, cut into bite-size strips
1/2   yellow pepper, cut into bite-size strips
1   medium red onion, sliced very thinly to make rings
  Green salad mix, your favorite
8   slices turkey bacon, crumbled, or soy bacon (optional)
6   circles of goat cheese (optional)
6   lime wedges (optional)

In a small bowl, combine the olive oil, vinegar, hot pepper sauce, salt and pepper, and thyme. Cut the shrimp crosswise into 1/2-inch pieces and toss with the dressing, then refrigerate. Marinate the shrimp in the dressing for at least 2 hours and the little crustaceans will absorb that wonderful Caribbean sun-drenched flavor.

To serve, place the salad mix on plates that have been chilled in the freezer. Place the shrimp and mango in the center of the salad, and circle the shrimp with the other ingredients. This is called a "composed salad," with the vegetables segregated into sections to create a dynamic presentation. If desired, garnish each plate with the crumbled bacon, and, if desired, a wedge of lime and a circle of goat cheese. No problem, mon! Serves 6.

Garbanzo Bean Salad

1   can garbanzo beans, drained and rinsed
1/2   chopped onion
1/4   cup freshly chopped parsley
3   carrots, unpeeled, diced and blanched
1   red bell pepper, diced
1/4   cup extra virgin olive oil
2   tablespoons cider vinegar
  Sea salt and cracked pepper to taste
1/2   cup chopped green or Greek olives

2   hard-cooked eggs, chopped
    Low-fat mayonnaise
    Romaine lettuce leaves or mixed field greens

Drain and rinse the beans. (The canning juices are loaded with salt, and if left on the beans will make this nutrient-dense dish gooey and unappetizing.) Combine the beans with the remaining ingredients except the lettuce or greens, and refrigerate.

To serve, mound this tasty mixture on a bed of romaine or field greens. Serves 6.

Chicken Salad

2   pounds boneless, skinless chicken breast halves
1   bay leaf
2   stalks celery, diced
1   small onion, chopped
$1/2$ cup grated carrot
$1/2$ cup low-fat mayonnaise
1   tablespoon Dijon mustard
$1/8$ teaspoon poultry seasoning
1   teaspoon chicken base
    Pinch of black pepper

In simmering water with a bay leaf, cook chicken breasts until done. Let cool, then chop up the chicken into pea-size bits. Combine chicken with remaining ingredients; mix and chill.

When assembling sandwiches, place lettuce on both sides of the bread to prevent the bread from getting too moist and gooey. Serves 8.

Alternate serving suggestions: This salad is great stuffed into a fresh-off-the-vine summer tomato. Make open-faced tea sandwiches and garnish with a grape cherry tomato half set over a leaf of basil.

Add halved grapes and some toasted nuts for a feminine-looking salad platter presentation. Or, place a 4-ounce scoop of chicken salad onto a bed of dark, leafy greens, then garnish with wedges of tomato, carrot and celery sticks, Greek olives, and strips of red bell pepper.

Beet Salad

As a child, I put beets on my list of hated vegetables, and only recently have I outgrown my aversion for this nutritionally rich, finger-staining root vegetable with its edible leaves (called chard).

Beets are worth spending time getting to know: One medium-size beet has only 50 calories, $^5/_{10}$ g fat, 2 g fiber, and 1 g protein. And you thought protein came only from animal products! Beets are also a good source of potassium and a fair source of vitamin A. And the beet greens—chard—are more nutritious than the beet itself. When you shop, buy small beets; they're sweeter, more tender, and more nutritious.

2	bunches small beets
$^1/_4$	cup rice vinegar
2	tablespoons water
2	tablespoons caraway seeds
1	teaspoon Stevia powder or Sucanat
2	tablespoons minced red onion
1	teaspoon grated horseradish
$^1/_4$	teaspoon ground clove
$^1/_2$	teaspoon sea salt
$^1/_4$	teaspoon cracked black pepper
4	tablespoons vegetable oil
$^1/_4$	cup chopped fresh parsley

Wash beets (do not peel). Trim off the greens and reserve.

Place the beets in a medium saucepan and cover with salted water. Boil until the beets are tender and can be easily pierced with a fork. Peel and slice.

Combine the remaining ingredients to make a marinade. Pour it over the still-warm beets and let stand for several hours, stirring them up once and a while. Serve over a bed of greens. Serves 4.

ॐ

Sometimes we make things more complicated than necessary. On the surface, the best salad dressings are charmingly simple. But if good salad dressings are easy, how come they are so frustratingly difficult to come by?

Simplicity is the key. Anyone can master the trick of making a safe, sugar-free, homemade, trans-fat-free salad dressing that will have your family and guests raving and asking where you got this full-bodied classic nectar. It is ridiculously simple, and here are some tips as to how it's done:

- When using garlic, work it into a paste or chop it very finely.
- Don't use cheap vinegar. Spend a few extra coins for a good quality product. Also, the most common fault in salad dressing failure is too much vinegar.
- Use balsamic vinegar as a wonderful substitute for wine vinegar. The dressing won't be "classic French," but it will be delicious.
- Add freshly chopped basil from the garden for a real treat.
- Throw in other ingredients that suit your fancy. Be adventurous—life is short!
- Grab your favorite canning jar or plastic container with a tight seal to prepare the dressing. Combine all ingredients and shake. Leftover dressing will last for several weeks in the refrigerator.
- Pour the dressing over your chilled greens only when you're ready to serve. And remember—dress the salad, don't drown it.

There is an old saying —

> *It takes three men to make a salad dressing:*
> *A generous man to add the oil,*
> *A miser to add the vinegar, and*
> *A wise man to add the seasonings.*

Classic French Vinaigrette

2½ cups extra virgin olive oil
1 cup red wine vinegar

3 cloves fresh garlic, minced
1 tablespoon Dijon mustard
Sea salt and cracked black pepper to taste

Combine all ingredients. Use immediately or store in the fridge.

Green Tea Vinaigrette

1 cup very strongly brewed green tea (3 bags per 8-ounce cup)
2 tablespoons rice vinegar
1 teaspoon soy sauce
1 teaspoon toasted sesame oil
1 teaspoon toasted sesame seeds
1 teaspoon honey or Sucanat
Crushed red pepper to taste

Whisk all ingredients together in a small bowl and chill out.

Ginger-Glazed Carrots and Peas

6 large carrots
12 ounces frozen peas
2 teaspoons cornstarch
1 tablespoon real maple syrup
2 teaspoons low sodium organic soy sauce
½ cup water
2 teaspoons extra virgin olive oil
2 cloves garlic, crushed
1 tablespoon minced fresh ginger
Sea salt and pepper
2 tablespoons toasted sesame seeds

Scrub the carrots (don't peel!) and cut them into coins. Steam them in a steamer basket over simmering water for 10 minutes and keep warm.

Steam the peas for about 2 minutes. Toss carrots and peas together in mixing bowl and keep warm.

Stir together the cornstarch and syrup in a small mixing bowl. Add the soy sauce and water and stir until smooth.

Heat a small sauté pan over medium heat, add olive oil, garlic, and ginger. Sauté till tender and fragrant, about 3 minutes. Add the soy sauce mixture to the sauté pan and simmer, stirring, for about 1 minute. Blast on high heat for 30 seconds, then remove the pan from the heat.

Season steamed vegetables with salt and pepper to taste. Pour the sauce over the vegetables, sprinkle with toasted sesame seeds, and serve with pride. Serves 6.

Sweet and Pungent Vegetables

Try to cut the veggies the same size for this dish.

2   cups diced unpeeled carrots
1   cup chopped onions
5   cups broccoli florets
2   cups diced red bell pepper
1   cup diced green bell pepper
1   cup sliced shiitake mushrooms
1   cup chopped celery
3   tablespoons unhydrogenated vegetable oil
2   tablespoons minced ginger
2   tablespoons minced garlic
    Sea salt and pepper
    Soy sauce
3   cups Sweet and Pour Sauce (page 144)
2   tablespoons toasted sesame seeds for garnish

Blanch the vegetables for 2 minutes in boiling water. Immediately plunge them into an ice bath. This is called "shocking" and it helps preserve the veggies' bright color. Drain very thoroughly (or the dish will become waterlogged).

Add oil, ginger, and garlic to a large pot over medium heat. When garlic and ginger begin to sizzle add the drained vegetables, toss, and sauté for about 1 minute. Season with salt and pepper and soy sauce to taste.

Add the Sweet and Pungent Sauce and toss to coat. Place in serving bowl and garnish with toasted sesame seeds. Serves 10.

Roasted Vegetables

Roasting is my favorite method enjoying vegetables, since the simple process intensifies the natural flavors.

$\frac{1}{4}$ cup olive oil
2   tablespoons minced garlic
$\frac{1}{2}$ teaspoon sea salt
$\frac{1}{2}$ teaspoon coarse black pepper
$1\frac{1}{2}$ pounds butternut squash, peeled
3   sweet potatoes, unpeeled
$1\frac{1}{2}$ pounds carrots, unpeeled
$1\frac{1}{2}$ pounds yellow onions, peeled and quartered
$1\frac{1}{2}$ pounds of red and green bell peppers, seeded and quartered
$\frac{1}{4}$ cup fresh thyme leaves, washed and stemmed
1   tablespoon balsamic vinegar

Preheat oven to 425 degrees.

Cut squash, sweet potatoes, and carrots into 1-inch cubes. Arrange those, and the onions and peppers, on a large baking pan.

Combine the olive oil, balsamic vinegar, garlic, salt, and pepper in a small bowl. Pour half of the mixture over the veggies and toss to coat, then place the veggies into the anxiously awaiting oven. (Place the vegetables that take longer to cook on the outside of the pan and the ones that take the least time in the center.) Roast the tasty morsels for 15 minutes, stir and turn. Roast another 15 minutes, and stir again. When the veggies are fork tender, they're done.

Toss the veggies in the remaining olive oil mix, add the thyme and balsamic vinegar and gently mix. Serves 10.

Stuffed Tomatoes with Mashed Basil-Potatoes

4   pounds Yukon Gold potatoes
8   large, fresh summer tomatoes
6   scallions, finely minced
3   tablespoons ground flax seed
2   tablespoons Dijon mustard
2   cloves of garlic, minced
½   cup Asiago or soy Parmesan cheese
2   bunches of fresh basil leaves, cut in a chiffonade (reserve some for garnish)

Prepare potatoes as Smashed Potatoes (page 15).

Slice off the tops of the tomatoes then scoop out the insides with a spoon or an ice cream scoop. Season the insides of the tomatoes with salt and pepper then invert them onto a dish towel to drain. When drained, slice a very small sliver off the bottom to keep them upright when they're filled.

While potatoes are still warm, mix with the onions, flax seed, mustard, garlic, cheese, and basil. Place the drained tomatoes on a sheet pan, open side up. With a spoon or pastry bag, fill the tomatoes with the warm potato mixture.

Bake at 400 degrees for 15 minutes or until potatoes begin to brown on top. Garnish with more chopped basil. Serves 8.

CHAPTER FIVE

Pasta

How about using the old noodle? Is there anybody out there who doesn't like pasta?

Spaghetti, macaroni, noodles, fettuccini, dumplings, soba noodles, rice sticks, ditali, penne, dim sum, lasagna, udon, orzo, and couscous. They're all *delicioso*!

The origins of pasta are unclear, but no matter what you call them, those muti-shaped forms of pressed grain flours are deeply rooted in world cultures, easy to prepare, and impossible to resist.

The humble noodle can be seen as a symbol of the democratizing influence of food. It's spread around the globe, stimulating interest in culinary ethnicity. And everybody likes it!

Noodles can be eaten hot or cold. Virtually any flour can be used—durum wheat, unbleached white flour, spelt, corn, garbanzo, whole wheat, rice, buckwheat—and all are perfectly compatible with any protein or vegetable treatment. Pasta is the perfect go-to health food, attractive to young and old, rich and poor alike. It should be emphasized here that we should cut back or totally avoid consuming processed white-flour pasta and explore the wide world of whole-grain pasta. And remember, egg noodles contain cholesterol.

Why condemn bleached white flour? Most naturopaths will present documentation showing that eating too many white foods can compromise our health. For example, white processed flour contains aluminum-based anticaking agents, along with the bleach used in processing. White foods, including white flour and white rice, are all simple starches which your body recognizes as sugar. These foods are devoid of nutrients. It is important to remember that every mouthful counts.

Uncle Ben did us no favors by converting his rice and removing the endosperm, which contains the bran and the majority of human health-enhancing nutrients. He downsized nature's rice from an energy-giving complex carbohydrate to a simple starch. Whole grains, in their natural unprocessed state, metabolize better and slower, providing us with stamina and energy. That's why marathoners carbo-load before the big race.

Many Americans may not know all this, but they do know they love pasta. The frequency at which U.S. consumers eat pasta products is high: 31 percent eat it three times a week, 46 percent once or twice a week, 17 percent once or twice a month, and 6 percent less often.

I will never forget the flavor of my first bowl of properly prepared Italian pasta. Enlightenment came slowly. As a penniless hippie in Boston during the "Summer of Love" I lived on a multitude of simple, feebly prepared homemade pasta dishes using various jarred tomato sauces, mayonnaise, or butter, and a green container of not-so-good Parmesan cheese. For me it was affordable, filling, and fun to eat.

Then, one of my friends rescued me and introduced me to Boston's North End, the Italian section right outside Haymarket Square, and my life changed forever. The tantalizing aroma of garlic hung in the air and scented the entire neighborhood like an exotic perfume. I was captivated by the Italian life and the endlessly different dishes using fresh tomatoes, virgin olive oil, tons of fresh garlic, anchovies, peppers, onions, mushrooms, Asiago, and mozzarella—MAMA MIA!

Living in Indiana most of my life had not afforded me a truly inspiring pasta dish, other than my old buddy Chef Boyardee, *à la* can. Bottled Italian dressing crowned the plain old iceberg lettuce salads, which accompanied plates of mushy, overcooked spaghetti (we'd never heard of "pasta" at that time) smothered with tomato sauce, no olive oil, and greasy ground beef with very little imagination applied to the seasonings or technique. We boiled the noodles till they were softer than a baby's bottom, and we'd often sauce it with ketchup or toss it with melted butter and Parmesan. Chef Boyardee was king and canned ravioli and SpaghettiOs the ruling princes.

And then, as if my world had not rocked enough in Boston, I soon discovered that several short blocks away stood the welcoming gates of Chinatown, with streets lined with dozens of Asian restaurants—each with its own regional specialty, most notably, slurpy, delicious noodles. Nothing comforted this naive little homesick Hoosier boy more than a steamy bowl of Chang House Restaurant's slurpy noodles. For as little as two and a half dollars you could fill your tummy and still have enough left over to take home for breakfast. (Of course, that was over thirty years ago.)

Later, I discovered these most delightful little restaurants serving dim sum appetizers, or as some called them, Chinese raviolis. We'd always walk up and down the streets and pick the one restaurant with the most Asian customers dining there, because we felt that if the locals supported them it must be authentic and more than likely served the best food.

Many long leisurely afternoons were spent at a dim sum house where my friends and I would proceed to participate in a three-hour dim sum and sake orgy, sucking down steamed dumplings like hungry pythons in a bunny cage. The cart would roll by and we'd inquire of the waitress, " What's in this one?" and she would say, "You no wanna know, you jus' eat." There was more than one instance where I could swear there was an eye looking back at me from inside a translucent, mouth-watering dumpling. But who cared? The flavors were intoxicating.

So, who invented pasta?

Greek mythology suggests that the god Hephaestus invented a device that made strings of dough, perhaps an early form of spaghetti. For years I innocently assumed that it certainly had to have been the Italians, since the existence of their empire goes back thousands of years and Italy is the home of wonderful pasta. Wrong! Legend would have us believe that Marco Polo introduced pasta to Italy following his explorations of the Far East late in the thirteenth century. He was only franchising the fast food of the day—original headquarters, China. The history of pasta can be traced back to China over 3000 years ago, where there is written evidence of a dried noodle-type food. Still, there is record of a lasagna-type product in Italy during Etruscan times. Some say that *maccheroni* is derived from the Sicilian word *maccarruni*, meaning "made into a dough by force."

The need to dry pasta, which had been eaten freshly-made for centuries, came with the increased trading that resulted from the establishment of the marine republics in Venice, Genoa, Pisa, and Amalfi. So, in the thirteenth century dried pasta was born; it could easily be stored on board ship for long voyages. In the fifteenth century the first recipe for lasagna was written by Father Bartolomea Secchi in his work *De Honesta Voluptate*, and in other recipes he also mentions long hollow pasta.

Now let's jump to the late seventeenth century, when the word "macaroni" came to America from England at the time of the American Revolution and ended up in an everlastingly popular song, "Yankee Doodle." This young patriot "went to town, riding on a pony. Stuck a feather in his cap and called it macaroni." Apparently, in England, the word "macaroni" meant perfection and elegance, usually in an affected sense. It was cool, man, cool. In other words, when the English soldier wrote the song about Yankee Doodle sticking a feather in his cap, that feather made him a fashionable dude. The cool Italian meaning came from the fact that most of the Italian fops (dudes) ate macaroni.

Here are some tips, with an emphasis on Mediterraneanizing the pasta, or serving it light:

- There is no truth to the fact that you need to add oil to the pasta's cooking water. It does help prevent the water from boiling over, but pass the oil by, pass it by.
- Use a large pot and generally five quarts of water for each pound of pasta. Don't scrimp on water. If pasta doesn't get enough room to move around, it gets really soggy, bummed out, and sticks together in starchy clumps.
- Don't overcook the pasta. Pasta is best when it's cooked *al dente*, or where it's done but still has plenty of texture when you bite into it (you'll have to pull a strand out after several minutes of cooking to check doneness). This requires some experimentation, but it's worth it. Pasta cooked this way is also better for you.
- Stir frequently, especially at first. There is a force called

spaghettal gravity and one can actually burn pasta. Believe me, I know.

- Save time by covering the pot. This will speed the cooking time and save on energy. You don't necessarily need to cook the pasta on high heat, either. That is when the trouble begins.

- Chop leftover cooked pasta, toss lightly with olive oil, and press into pie shells. Bake for three minutes at 375 degrees and fill your pasta crust with chili, meat sauce, or egg and cheese mixtures, and bake for a hot pasta pie.

- Save leftover pasta and toss it into soups for an entree with personality. Or, save leftover pasta, add onion, egg or liquid egg substitute, salt and pepper, and a little flour to make little fried pasta pancakes. Just like a potato pancake, put a little olive oil in a sauté pan and brown the patties on both sides until crispy.

- Most important, introduce yourself to the wide world of whole-grain pasta for which our appetites seem inexhaustible.

It was the Italians who said that pasta is like poetry. For nearly four hundred years they kept the secret of pasta, while making it into over three hundred shapes and countless recipes. They love it so much that in Pontedassio, Italy, they have created the Museo Storico Delgi Spaghetti, a pasta museum.

Good Oils vs. Bad Oils

At the end of this chapter are some simple and delicious pasta recipes, which have become favorites around our professional and personal kitchen. With your pasta, you may wish to serve one of the delicious green, leafy salads in the previous chapter, along with little saucers or bowls of oil for dipping whole-wheat focaccia bread slices. Oil is closely related to pasta in the Italian mind. But which oil to use for most healthy living?

We in the nutritional cooking industry have always touted olive oil. We have already sung the praises of the Mediterranean diet mentioned earlier in the book, and olive oil is at its heart.

After olive oil, we touted canola, praising the unsaturated fat aspect of this oil. Recent articles suggest that apparently we all didn't do our homework. We've been lulled, through advertising, into believing it to be perfectly safe. Alas, I, too, swallowed the line and sought out and purchased any product containing canola, snarfed it down trustingly, proclaiming it safe and healthy.

The case against hydrogenated oils—cottonseed, soy, peanut, and corn—was clear. They are molecularly changed oils that are toxic to the body. "For the record, research has conclusively shown that hydrogenated oils/trans-fats cause Type II non-insulin dependent diabetes, or hyperinsulinemia. This charged-up, molecularly altered oil dramatically increases risk of coronary heart disease, breast cancer, and other types of cancers and autoimmune diseases." (*Food for Thought: Hydrogenated Oils—Silent Killers*, by David Lawrence Dewey.)

So the health industry turned to the highly praised canola oil. Now it seems that the praises reported for canola really are propaganda put forth by the Canadian government because canola is one of that nation's chief export products. (The name canola is coined from the words "Canada" and "oil.")

Olive oil comes from olives, peanut oil from peanuts, and sunflower oil from sunflower seeds, but where does canola oil come from? The answers are startling. Rapeseed oil, which is really the name of the oil we call canola, comes from a genetically engineered plant, a weed of the mustard family, developed in Canada, which is usually considered toxic. Its most common form goes into lubricating oil used by small industry and has never been meant for consumption.

Canola oil has also been linked to lung cancer. According to an article in the *Wall Street Journal* (June 7, 1995), a study of stir-frying in China found canola to emit a cancer-causing chemical during the cooking process, especially when the oil began to smoke. Further studies with lab animals were disastrous. Rats developed fatty degeneration of the heart, kidneys, and adrenal and thyroid glands. When canola was withdrawn from their diets, the deposits dissolved, but scar tissue remained on all the affected organs. So, bon appetite to you—without canola! (But if you still want to use canola oil, get the safer expeller-pressed type.)

On the other hand, the good news is that there are wonderful alternative oils. Beyond the wonderful olive oil are other good choices: unprocessed sesame oil, soybean oil, walnut oil, corn oil, fish oils, and flax seed oil.

We need some fat for nutrition. That's the plain and simple truth and don't let anybody tell you otherwise. Fat adds rich flavor and a smooth texture to food and has a good "mouth feel," so we love it. But fat is also the most fattening source of energy: This lubricating substance contains nine calories per gram versus four calories per gram for carbohydrates and protein.

The amazing human body can produce most of the fat it needs, but dietary fat also supplies us with the fat-soluble vitamins A, D, E, and K, as well as essential fatty acids and arachidonic acids, which can't be synthesized by the body.

We have already said that saturated, or animal, fat can be harmful. Processed foods and dairy products are usually full of saturated fats, which raise blood cholesterol.

My advice is simple and effective. Put on those bifocals when you grocery shop and become a label reader. Ask questions of the management. If food suppliers hear enough complaints, they will make positive changes that will make navigating the sea of oil effortless.

Eat Right Recipes

PASTA

User-Friendly Fettuccini Alfredo

8	ounces fettuccini noodles
3	tablespoons extra virgin olive oil
1	cup evaporated milk
$1/2$	cup nonfat cream cheese
$3/4$	cup grated fresh Parmesan cheese*
$1/4$	teaspoon nutmeg
	Sea salt and black pepper

In a saucepan over very low heat, combine the evaporated milk and the cream cheese. Blend by stirring gently. Stir in the Parmesan, nutmeg, and salt and pepper to taste. Don't let it boil, or the sauce will separate. Keep warm over low heat.

Meanwhile, cook and drain the fettuccini, and in a nonstick sauté pan, toss with the olive oil. Add the sauce and top with chopped fresh herbs, blanched broccoli, or other blanched vegetables as desired. Serve immediately. Serves 6.

Special note: If you wish, add small bite-size pieces of chicken, salmon, lean pork loin strips, or turkey breast to fulfill your meat needs. And remember—be happy when you cook, because your mood is in the food.

*Galaxy Foods makes an organic tofu Parmesan-flavored product that is terrific. No fat, but tons of flavor!

Broccoli Stuffed Shells

(Recipe courtesy of Deb McClure-Smith)

30   jumbo pasta shells
4   cups low-fat cottage cheese
2   cups shredded nonfat mozzarella cheese
1/2   cup grated Parmesan cheese
3/4   teaspoon oregano
1   10-ounce package frozen chopped broccoli, thawed
3/4   cup liquid egg substitute or 3 egg whites
1   32-ounce jar spaghetti sauce

Cook the pasta shells; drain, rinse, and set aside.

Combine cottage and mozzarella cheeses, 1/4 cup of the Parmesan cheese, and the egg substitute or egg whites and mix well. Blend in the oregano and broccoli.

Fill each shell with about 2 tablespoons of the cheese and broccoli mixture. Spread a thin layer of spaghetti sauce in 13 x 9-inch baking dish. Place the shells open side down in single layer. Cover with the remaining sauce. Sprinkle the remaining Parmesan cheese over the top. Cover with foil and bake at 350 degrees for 35 minutes. Serves 8.

Pasta with Garlic, Virgin Olive Oil, Crushed Red Pepper, and Parsley

2   pounds of your favorite pasta
1   cup extra virgin olive oil
1/4   cup minced fresh garlic
8   anchovy fillets, minced (or 2 tablespoons anchovy paste)
1   cup chopped parsley
1   teaspoon crushed red pepper
1   teaspoon coarse black pepper
2   tablespoons wheat germ

Cook the pasta in 10 quarts of water. Drain, rinse, and keep warm.

In a large sauté pan, heat oil over medium heat. Cook garlic until it softens, but not till it browns. Pull the pan off of the heat and mash the anchovies into oil mixture.

Next add the crushed red pepper, half of the parsley, and the black pepper. Add the pasta to the sauce. Gently toss to mix over low heat till warmed through. Add the wheat germ, and cook for 1 minute. Serve on warmed platter and garnish with the remaining parsley. Serves 8.

Sicilian Pasta

Whenever I make this mouth-watering, garlicky dish, my family and crew squeal with anticipation. It is simple, easy, and full of the sun-drenched flavors of southern Italy. The tomato concentrate gives the dish a deep, rich flavor and a big dose of cancer-preventing lycopene. The raw garlic added at the end of the cooking process will help keep your arteries flexible and vampires at bay. Have plenty of after-dinner mints on hand.

1	pound of your favorite whole-grain pasta
4	tablespoons olive oil
4	tablespoons fresh minced garlic
$1/2$	teaspoon coarse black pepper
$1/2$	teaspoon crushed red pepper
1	small can of tomato concentrate
	Sea salt
2	cups grated Asiago cheese

Cook the pasta *al denté*. Drain, rinse, and keep warm.

In a large, nonstick sauté pan, warm the oil over medium-high heat. Add 2 tablespooons of the garlic, the black pepper, crushed red pepper, and tomato concentrate. Simmer for 1 minute. Fill the empty tomato concentrate can with water to remove all the tomato goodies left inside, and then add it to the mixture. Reduce the heat to medium-low simmer for 1 minute, stirring.

Add the cooked, drained pasta to the sauce, along with the remaining garlic, and mix everything together. Gently, or you'll break up the pasta.

If the dish is too dry, add water, a little at a time. Toss with care. Add salt to taste.

Serve on a heated dinner plate and crown with the grated Asiago cheese. Serves 4.

Fowler's House Pasta

This classic blend of Mediterranean flavors has been a crowd pleaser for years. Serve at room temperature for best flavor.

1	pound pasta
1/2	cup virgin olive oil
4	tablespoons minced garlic
2	cups fresh tomatoes, skinned and chopped
1/4	cup capers, with juice
1	bunch scallions, minced
2	packages fresh basil, washed and chopped
	Sea salt and coarse black pepper
1	teaspoon cayenne pepper
1/4	cup rice vinegar
1/2	cup Parmesan cheese

Cook pasta. Drain, rinse, and keep warm.

In a large sauté pan, heat the olive oil over medium heat and sauté 2 tablespoons of the garlic. Pull off the heat and add the tomatoes, capers, scallions, basil, salt and pepper to taste, cayenne pepper, and vinegar.

In a large mixing bowl, combine the cooked pasta and the remaining garlic. Pour warm tomato mixture over the pasta and toss gently. Top with the Parmesan cheese and serve. Serves 4.

Slurpy Spicy Asian Lo Mein Noodles

1	pound whole-grain pasta, such as linguini, rice noodles, or soba or udon noodles.

½   cup water
2   tablespoons cornstarch
1   tablespoon toasted sesame oil
1   tablespoon chopped fresh garlic
1   tablespoon chopped fresh ginger
½   teaspoon cayenne pepper
½   cup toasted crushed peanuts
½   cup chopped each of: carrots, red and yellow peppers, broccoli
        and cauliflower florets, and snow peas.
½   cup soy sauce
1   tablespoon honey
3   scallions, chopped

Cook pasta till *al dente*. Drain and keep warm

Mix the water and cornstarch together to make a slurry.

In a nonstick skillet, heat the oil over medium heat and sauté the garlic, ginger, and cayenne pepper for 2 minutes. Add the peanuts and stir them around to get them warm.

Now add the carrots, peppers, broccoli, cauliflower, and snow peas, and stir-fry for 2 minutes. Don't walk away—you have to stir constantly!

Add the soy sauce, honey, and the slurry, and stir till the sauce thickens. Add the pasta and toss to coat. Garnish with chopped scallions and serve. Serves 4.

Special note: If you wish, add small pieces of raw chicken to step two and cook along with the ginger and garlic. Chicken, tempeh, pork, and seafood all work well with this mouth-pleasing dish.

Chapter Six

Luncheons — Hale, Hearty, and Nutritious

Lunch doesn't have to be a burger. A Mediterranean diet lunch, with pasta and vegetable salad and olive oil dip for whole-wheat focaccia, and a legume is tops in good nutrition. Hearty, lusty sandwiches, colorful luncheon entrées, and crunchy fresh salads can satisfy hunger while reinforcing nutrition for the energy your earth suit will need for the rest of the day.

Try concentrating on vegetable lunches—and I don't mean just a plate of spinach and garlicky mashed potatoes.

Vegetarians have long known that chopped, savory roasted or grilled vegetable combinations make great sandwiches. Try 'em yourself and give 'em to your kids, too.

Once you go in a vegetable direction, consider organic vegetables and fruits. They're increasingly popular for good reason, especially in the summer when farmers markets are popping up all around two-lane highways and byways. That fresh taste will make you rush home to cook and eat.

So you are the people tearing down the Brazilian rainforest and breeding cattle.

—Britain's Prince Philip
to McDonald's of Canada

Go Organic!

Cissy Bowman, a Hoosier organic farmer for many years, describes the intricacies of organic farming:

There are many good reasons for going organic, for a farmer or consumer. Most people are aware that organic food has been raised and handled without chemicals, but it's a lot more than that.

Acre by acre and plate by plate, organics is still changing the world. What was once called a niche market is now considered to be mainstream. By the late 1980s, the public became aware of organic foods: veggies, eggs, perhaps flour.

It would be accurate to say that organics has all but taken over my life since 1989, when the Organic Foods Production Act (OFPA) was written. In an effort to provide assurance to the people who bought organic food from my small farm I stumbled into the world of organic certification, which was pretty much unheard of in the Midwest back then. I met eight of Indiana's organic farmers at a meeting that July. I saw in them the same passion I felt for the land and for protecting consumers. We have certainly moved on since that organic foods act was passed by Congress. Now, eleven years after OFPA was passed, we are on the verge of seeing that act finally implemented.

Certification and professionalization make the industry grow. Today we see representatives from industry there—large corporations that want to jump on the organic bandwagon. They know that the market for certified organic food is world-wide and that there is a premium for it. Sales of organic food are increasing twenty-two percent a year in the U.S. alone.

According to the Organic Trade Association, the National Organic Program is moving ahead despite the tremendous issues it faces. The USDA accreditation process has begun and by October of

2002 we are scheduled to see the "USDA Organic" label on products. This label will mean that the product has been certified to meet the U.S. organic standard. In 2002 it also becomes illegal to sell a product as organic unless it is certified.

Organic farmers go through a lot of trouble to prove that they comply with the regulations. They keep records and documents and create an organic system plan that describes how they comply with the standards. In these days of concern about food safety, organic offers more than just Earth friendly methods. Organic products can be traced through an audit trail that follows the product from the field to the consumer. As one who is proud to be an organic farmer and who has been around this business for a long time, I can honestly say that almost all of the other growers I have met have great love and respect for the planet as well as the people who consume their crops. It's a personal thing they feel—a relationship—which they take very seriously. And I think that love is transmitted to the crops which are harvested and sold to the American public.

Cissy Bowman is a member of Hoosier Organic Marketing Education, a nonprofit, public benefit, educational, 501(c)3 organization dedicated to offering information about organic food, farming, standards, and markets since 1991. Her farm is located in Clayton, Indiana.

Luncheons

Polenta, Wendell Style

Polenta is one of our favorite side dishes, and when we add vegetables and cheese it is a hearty luncheon dish.

2 cups vegetable stock or defatted chicken stock
1 cup polenta cornmeal
1 tablespoon olive oil
2 tablespoons diced red pepper
2 tablespoons diced green chiles
2 tablespoons corn kernels
1 cup grated nonfat cheddar cheese or soy cheddar cheese
4 tablespoons Parmesan or soy Parmesan cheese
2 tablespoons wheat germ

In a nonreactive saucepan bring the stock to a boil over high heat. Slowly pour the cornmeal into the boiling stock in a steady, fine stream, whisking briskly to prevent lumping. Reduce the heat to medium. With a wooden spoon, stir constantly. The mixture will gradually thicken.

Add the remaining ingredients and continue to cook, stirring, for another 5 minutes. Remove from heat, cover, and let stand for 5 minutes before serving.

Special note: If you want to be naughty—and it's okay to be naughty once and a while—add a pat of butter and a little shredded Gruyère cheese and top with a spoonful of your favorite tapanade.

Vegetable and Brown Rice Salad

$1/2$	cup lemon juice
4	tablespoons Dijon mustard
2	cups vegetable stock
$1/4$	cup extra virgin olive oil
$1/2$	teaspoon sea salt
1	teaspoon coarse black pepper
2	pounds zucchini squash
8	stalks celery
4	carrots
2	cups cooked brown rice
2	bunches arugula, stemmed and finely chopped
1	yellow or red bell pepper, diced
1	bunch scallions, chopped finely
1	cup chopped parsley

In a mixing bowl, whisk together the lemon juice, mustard, vegetable stock, oil, salt, and pepper.

Wash zucchini, celery, and carrots thoroughly and cut into $1/4$-inch dice. (Leave the skins on since much of the nutrition resides there.) Add the rice and remaining ingredients. Mix well with a fork, not a spoon. This is best served at room temperature. Serves 10.

Barley and Black Walnut Pilaf

3	cups either vegetable or chicken stock
$1/4$	cup dry white wine
1	cup pearled barley
$1/2$	cup toasted black walnut pieces
$1/4$	cup vegetable or chicken stock
$1/2$	cup raisins
1	clove garlic, minced
1	stalk celery, diced
1	carrot with skin, diced
1	red bell pepper, diced
3	scallions, chopped

1/2   cup chopped fresh parsley
      Several drops of black walnut extract
      Sea salt and black pepper to taste.

In a medium nonreactive saucepan, bring the stock and wine to a boil. Add the barley and reduce heat to low. Cover and cook for about 50 minutes or until barley is tender.

In a nonstick skillet, toast the black walnut pieces over medium-high heat for 2 minutes. Don't walk away. Reduce the heat to medium and add 1/4 cup stock to the pan, then add the raisins, garlic, celery, carrot, and pepper. Simmer for about 1 minute. Leave the veggies a little crisp to preserve their nutrients.

Combine the vegetable with the nut mixture and barley. Add the parsley and scallions and mix well. Add walnut extract and salt and pepper to taste. Serves 6.

Special note: Add chicken, tempeh, or lean cuts of meat to this dish early in the sauté process to turn this into a hearty luncheon entrée.

Grilled Veggie Sandwiches

4   tablespoons extra virgin olive oil
1   tablespoon rice vinegar
4   whole-wheat hamburger buns
4   slices each of red onion and tomato, cut 1/4-inch thick
1   large portobello mushroom, cleaned and stemmed.
1   large red bell pepper and 1 large yellow bell pepper
8   large spinach leaves
    Sea salt and pepper to taste
2   cloves garlic, minced
    Grated tofu cheddar cheese or nonfat shredded cheddar

Combine the olive oil, vinegar, and garlic in a mixing bowl. Brush some of the mixture on the cut sides of the buns.

Toss the vegetables and mushroom with the remaining oil mixture and marinate for at least 1 hour.

Arrange the vegetables, except the spinach, on the grilling rack. Grill about 5–6 minutes, then turn and grill another 5–6 minutes. During the last few minutes of cook time, toast the buns.

Arrange the spinach on the oiled side of the bread and top with the grilled onion rings and tomato slices. Cut the mushroom into four triangular pieces, and place a piece on each sandwich. Arrange the remaining vegetables evenly. Sprinkle with cheese and serve. Serves 4.

Millet Burgers with Shiitake Mushrooms

1	tablespoon extra virgin olive oil
8	shiitake caps, cut into thin julienne strips
	Pinch of crushed red pepper
3	cups cooked millet
3/4	cup each of grated carrot and minced onion
1/4	cup freshly chopped parsley
3/4	cup organic whole-wheat flour
1	teaspoon sea salt
2	tablespoons mushroom soy sauce
2	teaspoons extra virgin olive oil

In a nonstick skillet over medium-high heat, heat 1 tablespoon of olive oil, then toss in the mushrooms and crushed red pepper. Sauté for 4 minutes.

In a mixing bowl, combine the millet, mushrooms, carrot, onion, parsley, flour, and mushroom soy sauce. Mix thoroughly and refrigerate for 1 hour.

To cook, form the mixture into patties. In a nonstick skillet over medium-high heat, heat 2 teaspoons of olive oil and cook the patties 4–5 minutes per side, or till golden.

Special note: Of course, these make great sandwiches. The millet patties can also be served as an entrée by topping them with nonfat gravy. Serve along with a fresh vegetable, a salad, and some grain bread for a familiar dinner format. They can also be served over a bed of Smashed Potatoes and then topped with gravy to make a "Millet Manhattan."

Tempeh Sloppy Joes

2   tablespoons extra virgin olive oil
1   package tempeh
1/4 cup each diced carrot, green pepper, and celery
1   medium onion, chopped
4   tablespoons wheat germ
1   can of chili sauce
4   tablespoons balsamic vinegar
1   teaspoon cinnamon
    Splash of hot sauce
1   teaspoon Stevia powder
2   tablespoons soy sauce or Worcestershire sauce
2   cups cooked brown rice

In a nonstick skillet over medium heat, heat the olive oil. Add the tempeh and break it up with the back of a fork or spoon until it's in little nibs. Sauté until the tempeh is browned.

Add the rest of the ingredients, except the rice, and simmer for 1 minute, stirring frequently. Add the rice and mix thoroughly and simmer for 5 minutes. If it becomes too dry, add a bit of water to thin. Serve on whole-wheat buns. Serves 6.

Veggie Burgers

3 1/2 cups water
1/2 cup pearled barley
1/2 cup brown rice
1/2 cup brown lentils
4   tablespoons olive oil
1 1/2 cups chopped carrots
3/4 cup each chopped onion, celery, and broccoli
2   tablespoons chopped brazil nuts or almonds
3   cloves garlic, minced
1/4 cup fresh basil, minced
1   tablespoon fresh oregano, minced

2 teaspoons sea salt
3 egg whites
1 cup organic whole-wheat flour
2 tablespoons olive oil
   Leaf lettuce leaves
   Sliced tomatoes and red onion

In a large saucepan, bring the water to a boil. Stir in the barley, rice, and lentils. Bring to a boil and reduce heat. Cover and simmer 40–45 minutes or until lentils and grains are tender. Add more water if needed. Drain the excess liquid and let cool.

Heat 2 tablespoons of olive oil in a large skillet over medium-high heat. Add the carrots, celery, onion, broccoli, nuts, and garlic. Cook, stirring, 4–5 minutes. Stir in the basil, oregano, and salt, and transfer to a mixing bowl. Chill overnight for best results.

Before cooking the grain and veggie mixture, stir in the egg whites and flour. Moisten your hands and form twelve 3/4-inch-thick patties.

Grab a large nonstick skillet and heat up the remaining 2 tablespoons of olive oil over medium fire. Carefully place the patties in the skillet and cook about 10–12 minutes or until golden brown and thoroughly done in the middle. Serve on whole-wheat buns with lettuce, tomato, and onion slices.

Special note: Taste the sandwich before you go slapping on mayonnaise, mustard, or ketchup. The sandwich stands alone. Toast your buns first for best results.

Tofu "Egg" Salad

1   container of organic extra-firm silken tofu
1/4 cup finely minced onion
1   stalk of chopped celery
    Pinch of fresh parsley
1/2 cup low-fat mayonnaise
2   tablespoons Chicken and Egg Salad Seasoning Mix (recipe
       follows)

$^1/_2$ teaspoon turmeric

Combine all ingredients and mix well. Adjust seasonings to taste. Serve on sandwiches or with greens or fruit.

Chicken and Egg Salad Seasoning Mix

1   cup organic nutritional yeast flakes
1   tablespoon turmeric
1   tablespoon celery salt
1   tablespoon onion powder
2   teaspoons garlic powder
$^1/_4$ teaspoon white pepper

This highly nutritional spice mix can also be used on soups and vegetable dishes. Store in your pantry in an airtight container.

Tempeh Reuben

2   tablespoons soy sauce (or tamari or Bragg Liquid Aminos*)
1   teaspoon garlic powder
1   teaspoon onion powder
$^1/_2$ teaspoon caraway seed
$^1/_2$ teaspoon celery seed
1   tablespoon rice vinegar
1   teaspoon nutritional yeast
$^2/_3$ cup water
    Sea salt and black pepper
1   package multigrain organic tempeh
    Good quality rye bread
    Lowfat Swiss cheese or soy Swiss cheese
    Sauerkraut (squeezed dry)
    Low-fat or nonfat Russian or 1000 Island Dressing

Make a marinade by mixing the soy sauce (or tamari or Liquid Aminos), garlic and onion powders, caraway and celery seed, vinegar, nutritional yeast, water, and salt and pepper to taste in a shallow dish.

Cut the tempeh in half, then slice each half horizontally to make 4 pieces. Add the tempeh to the marinade and refrigerate for several hours. (If you are in a big rush, an hour should do it. Just make sure you turn the tempeh over a few times so the flavor will permeate the entire piece of tempeh.)

Remove the tempeh from the marinade and cut in half, then cut each half horizontally so you have 4 pieces.

Lightly coat a nonstick sauté pan with nonstick spray and warm over medium heat. Add the tempeh and brown on both sides.

Assemble the sandwich as follows: On a piece of rye, place a slice of cheese, some sauerkraut, a piece of tempeh, and another piece of cheese, finishing with a piece of rye bread. Place in a skillet and toast, much as you would a grilled cheese. Add salad dressing to suit your taste. Serves 4.

  * Found in most whole food stores.

Tempeh "Meatball" Subs

1   8-ounce package multigrain organic tempeh
2   tablespoons extra virgin olive oil
1   10-ounce jar marinara sauce
1   green pepper, sliced thinly
1   medium onion, sliced thinly
4   tablespoons grated Parmesan or tofu Parmesan cheese
1   tablespoon dried oregano

Cut the tempeh into 1-inch cubes. Heat the olive oil in a nonstick sauté pan over medium-high heat. Add the tempeh and cook for 10 minutes turning frequently to ensure all sides get browned sufficiently.

Toward the end of the browning process add the onions and peppers. Cook for two minutes more. Reduce heat to low, and add the marinara and oregano. Serves 4.

&

Chapter Seven

Not-quite Vegetarian — Nonvegetarian Entrées

I've been a caterer for years, supplying fancy food for weddings, parties, special office events, and private home soirées. Naturally, not all of my customers wished vegetarian offerings, so I've prepared all types of foods, depending on the customer's personal preferences. I'm including some philosophy, menu tips, and recipes for those who aren't as yet converted.

We focused on luncheon dishes in the previous chapter. Now we're going to center our discussion on the family dinner table, and especially on the entrée that sets the pace for the rest of the meal. These nonvegetarian recipe offerings have been carefully screened to insure their nutritional and safe-eating value even though they do contain meat. My suggestions are derived from nutritionists at hospitals that emphasize heart-safe and healthy diets for their patients. These hospital diets emphasize the USDA Food Pyramid, which is a better guide to eating than just "hand-to-mouth," the diet many Americans are observing. The Mediterranean diet also works well for nonvegetarians. It makes wonderful and artistic evening dinners possible.

There are many things to consider when developing healthy eating patterns for nonvegetarians who are considering meal choices at dinnertime, when entrées generally are served. Culture, family background, religion, moral beliefs, the cost and availability of food, individual preferences, food intolerances, and allergies are all factors in dietary habits. The food pyramid does provide a structure that can be adapted to all these factors. For example, if you choose to avoid one or two food groups, you can still get these nutrients from other categories of food on the pyramid. For those who choose to avoid dairy products, targeting other food groups with calcium is important. If you avoid all or most animal products, be sure to choose foods high in iron, vitamin B12, calcium, and zinc.

Eating out and eating healthy can be difficult. There are so many choices, and many of them aren't good. Americans are assaulted with gigantic plates full of food when they dine out. The restaurant can charge more for huge plates of food, but the industry has yet to focus on what's good for the American eating public. The focus is on the bottom line—profit.

Select small portion sizes and share entrées or take leftovers home. When eating out, ask questions regarding food preparation. Looking at a full day's nutrition, limit portion sizes of the entrée, and also of foods high in calories such as cookies, cakes and other sweets, french fries, fats, oils, and spreads. Avoid adding salt to your food, because the sodium content is often already high.

Food nutritional awareness begins in the kitchen, long before the entrée and its accompaniments reach the dinner table. Reading food labels is essential for healthy eating. Food labels contain several parts including the front panel, ingredient list, and nutrition facts. The front panel tells you if nutrients have been added, such as iodine in iodized salt or thiamin, riboflavin, niacin, iron, and folic acid in enriched pasta. The ingredients list also lets you know what is in the food, such as fats or sugars. The ingredients are listed in descending order by weight. The nutrition facts will tell you the content of the food's nutrients and the percentage of daily value a portion contains. If you want to eat more of a nutrient, choose foods with a higher percentage value of it. As a general guide, foods with 5 percent or less of daily value contribute only a small amount of that nutrient to your diet. Nutrients with 20 percent or more contribute a larger amount of that item to your diet

Many people have vitamin bottles sitting near their plates at the dinner table. They take daily dietary supplements. Vitamins can be very important to pregnant women who need more folic acid or older adults who are not exposed to sunlight and need vitamin D. People who do not eat dairy products may need a calcium supplement. Those who do not eat animal products may need to take a vitamin B12 supplement. However, it is not advisable to depend on supplements to meet your usual nutrient needs because foods contain many substances that promote health that cannot be obtained from a supplement. However, large amounts of nutrients such as vitamin A and selenium can be harmful, according to the USDA, which supplies these statistics and recommendations each year.

We already have talked about the importance of cutting fat in the diet. Keep remembering it, every time you put fork to mouth.

Consuming less salt is a very important factor in maintaining a heart healthy diet. Sodium is the major component of salt, and many studies have shown high sodium intake is associated with high blood pressure. To reduce sodium intake, choose and prepare foods with less salt and eat lots of fruits and vegetables, which are naturally low in salt—and calories. Most of the sodium you eat comes from foods that have salt added during food processing or preparation in a restaurant or at home. Use herbs and spices to flavor foods instead of salt. Read food labels and choose foods that have 140 mg of sodium or less per serving (considered low sodium). Remember, condiments such as soy sauce, ketchup, mustard, pickles, and olives can add a lot of sodium to your diet.

Since you're preparing a dinner with meat, let's talk about how to cook it in a healthful way. We'll start with poultry.

I can't criticize those who still wish to cook a turkey for Thanksgiving, though turkeys do have moms. But let's at least do the roasting correctly and in as light a way as we can.

Tradition has taught us to simply preheat the oven, throw in the bird, and cook the gobble out of it until it's done. There's so much more to add to that old "war-horse" cooking method. Over the years, chefs have discovered some simple techniques to improve turkey and render it tender, moist, and full of flavor. Allow me to share those tips.

Select an 11- to 14-pound turkey. If the bird is frozen, defrost in the refrigerator two days prior to cooking. Plan to cook it the day before the meal. That's right—the day before. While defrosting, place a pan beneath it to prevent raw juices from dripping onto other foods, a serious cross-contamination problem.

When thawed, remove the giblet and liver package. Cook these innards and give them to the cat or dog. Use the neck for turkey stock.

If you have a fresh, free-range, minimally processed turkey, you may wish to brine it. To do that, find a clean plastic bucket large enough to hold the turkey. Make a brining solution by combining 1 cup of kosher or sea salt per gallon of water. Immerse the turkey, tail-end up, in the solution, making sure that it is as submerged as possible, and soak, refrigerated, for 12 to 15 hours. If you wish, you may add some herbs, such as rosemary or thyme, to the brining solution. (**Note:** Do not brine a frozen turkey from the supermarket. Most of those turkeys have been processed with quite a bit of salt already, and brining could render them inedible.)

Rinse the turkey and pat dry. Rub the outside with olive oil then sprinkle with sea salt, paprika, and black pepper. DO NOT STUFF THE BIRD! Leave the inner cavity of the carcass empty or place some onions and carrots inside. Without the density of the stuffing, the gobbler will cook much more quickly and you will be substituting tasty vegetables for the many calories and fat of stuffing. Tie the legs together and secure the wings with twine or toothpicks.

In a large roasting pan, place the turkey breast-side down on a V-rack. (You can purchase a V-rack at any restaurant supply house or at one of the gourmet food and kitchen utensil stores that exist in every mall across America. It's a worthwhile investment.) Pour about an inch of water and 2 cups of a good dry white wine in the pan. Arrange some cut up onion, carrots, celery, and garlic in the pan.

Preheat oven to 400 degrees and adjust the oven rack to the lowest position. Tent the turkey with foil and roast for 45 minutes. Remove the turkey from the oven and baste it with pan drippings. Add a little water if the roasting pan is beginning to go dry.

Using two clean dish towels, turn the turkey on its side, so that one leg and one wing are facing up. Return to the oven and cook for an additional 30 minutes.

Remove the turkey from the oven, and turn it breast-side up. (You'll turn the turkey only those two times; otherwise you risk having it fall apart.) Roast for another 35 minutes. While the turkey roasts, be sure to check the liquid level in the pan so the roasting vegetables don't burn or scorch.

To check for doneness, insert a meat thermometer in the thickest part of the turkey, usually the thigh. Be careful that the thermometer does not touch the bone. When the temperature reaches 170 degrees, and the juices run clear, you, and the turkey, are done.

As soon as the turkey has cooled enough to handle, remove the entire breast from the carcass in one piece, then remove the dark meat. Refrigerate the meat.

Once all the available meat is removed, place the bones and skin in a large stockpot with carrots, celery, onions, bay leaf, poultry seasoning, with a little chicken bouillon or base. Add water to cover and bring to a boil, then reduce the heat and simmer until you have a good broth. Strain.

Now you have some stock for the gravy and stuffing. Refrigerate the stock overnight. In the morning, you can skim off all of the disgusting fat that has congealed on the top of the stock. But don't give the fat to the dog or cat. Domestic animals suffer from the same diseases as humans.

Once your stock is defatted and ready, make your stuffing. Place it in a large baking pan, then place the sliced turkey over the top. Add more broth, wrap, and forget about it till thanksgiving morning. Wrap and refrigerate till you're ready to reheat and serve.

When making gravy, reduce the amount of saturated fat in the meal by using a cornstarch slurry instead of a butter and flour roux.

Having done the bulk of preparation the day before, you'll have more time to spend with your family!

There are turkey Web sites which will answer other questions you may have and offer helpful suggestions; just look under "turkey" on your browser.

From a computer analysis of a typical Thanksgiving dinner serving it has been determined that there are 2500 calories with 144 grams of fat and a whopping 120 mg of cholesterol. Most of the fat comes from the fatty stock and pan drippings. But you're going to defat the stock, right?

Chicken can be roasted in the same way as turkey, or sautéed in a small amount of olive oil or poached in broth, wine, or water.

If you are choosing to cook pork (you'll notice I don't even touch the preparation of beef in this book), be aware of these "small choice" improvements for your diet. Choose lean cuts of pork without marbled fat such as pork loin, tenderloin, or Canadian bacon. (Pork chops often are too fatty for good health.) Pork should be roasted slowly, at 325 degrees in a covered pan, which allows it to stay juicy while still draining away fat as it cooks. Pork medallions (from a tenderloin), which are to be sautéed, do not need to have extra skillet fat supplied. They'll supply their own juice.

So now the table is beautifully set, candles lit, and all have seated themselves to dine. Your nutrition-conscious food is beautifully presented on the good china, and guests have raised their wine and water glasses in a toast. Time for some good dinner table banter.

Why not make it on the subject of eating right? (Are there other subjects?) I don't know if it's polite to sit at the dinner table and say to friends gathered around, "Let's look at this dinner plate and the salad, too. I'd like to do a critique on whether the food on the plates is good, or bad, for your reputation as a lover. Do you realize that what you do in this dining room may affect what you do later in the bedroom? Ever since Adam and Eve—or was that Lilith?—waltzed through the Garden of Eden sharing a juicy apple, love affairs and food have gone hand in hand."

Your guests may frown and blush, but they may be interested in your comments. First supply them with a little background.

According to our eloquent researchers at *Encyclopedia Britannica*, delving studiously into the subject of food as an aphrodisiac: "[There is] a psycho physiological reaction that a well-prepared meal can have upon the human organism. The combination of various sensuous reactions—the visual satisfaction of the sight of appetizing food, the olfactory stimulation of their pleasing smells and the tactile gratification afforded the oral mechanism by rich, savory dishes—tends to bring on a state of general euphoria conducive to sexual expression." Took the words right out of my mouth.

The term aphrodisiac comes from "Aphrodite," the name of the Greek goddess of love and beauty. According to Richard Miller, author of *The Magical and Ritual Use of Aphrodisiacs,* these stimulating substances should do one or more of the following: improve sexual health, increase sexual awareness, relax inhibitions, arouse sexual feelings by stimulating the nervous system, augment physical energy, help conquer impotence and frigidity, and strengthen the glands involved with sex.

Casanova downed oysters and a cup of chocolate before venturing into a lady's boudoir. Montezuma II consumed fifty glasses of chocolate sweetened with honey to sustain his virility. Cleopatra seduced Mark Anthony in a scented, royal chamber knee-deep in rose petals. And it was believed that the spice cardamom, known as the "fire of Venus," created a magical effect on the opposite sex.

Since ancient times we've tried to boost our sexual libido through magic potions and foods such as oysters, chocolate, fish, truffles, and ginger. First, let's address the topic of everyone's favorite—chocolate. There are many delicious points to be addressed in the defense of chocolate. First, it feels so wonderfully seductive in the mouth. According to Deralee Scanlon, R.D., chocolate's reputation may be due to its abundant supply of phenylethylamine, an amphetamine-like chemical. Levels in our brains go up when we meet the right person. Chocolate also contains caffeine, which stimulates the release of epinephrine, one of the brain's messengers that triggers sexual response. Large doses of cocoa are believed to stimulate the production of the neurotransmitter serotonin, thus enhancing the feeling of being in love.

Now for your good and bad foods list for the lover:

- Avocados are storehouses of nutrients, high in potassium, phosphorous, sulphur, magnesium, and other elements. The avocado is credited with supplying energy.
- Carrots, or *philons*, as the ancient Greeks called them. *Philon* comes from the root word for "loving," reflecting the belief that the carrot had aphrodisiac power. Carrots supply an estrogen-like compound that stimulates the sexual appetite. Plus, eating carrots helps you see well in the dark. That's good under the circumstances, isn't it?
- Hot peppers stimulate your body's circulation. Good circulation is essential to good performance in bed.
- Garlic was widely used in ancient times among the Egyptians, Greeks, and Romans. The stinking rose is alleged to contain compounds related to sex hormones. Pass the mints, please.
- Shiitake mushrooms are known to have a positive effect on sexual strength in men and a stimulating effect on females. And all that is in addition to the shiitake's ability to stimulate the immune system.
- The Greeks used figs as their sensual favorite. Figs contain magnesium, which is essential for producing sex hormones as well as for improving your eyesight.
- The pomegranate, praised by D. H. Lawrence in *Women in Love*, has been touted as an aphrodisiac since Old Testament times.
- The apple is visually suggestive.

Here are some food suggestions lovers should note:

- Fatty meats are not macho, because science knows that saturated fats clog arteries impeding the flow of blood and circulation to the body's extremities.
- Butter is better in moderation than margarine, but olive oil is by far the best to keep you fit and trim.

- Too much wine or any alcohol may make you just *think* you're a good lover. Practice moderation.
- Illegal street drugs are a bummer.
- Stop smoking and cut down on the sugar intake.

Forgive me as I digress. Your guests around that dinner table are either dozing by now or ready to crown you with the butter plate.

You may all be excused from the table to call the pharmacist and cancel your Viagra prescriptions.

But truly the food you eat for dinner can affect your sex life and your overall health. Clearly, you have to breathe right to enjoy good health, and there's another lifestyle issue I'd like to talk about right here. Dinner's over, you reach for—the after-dinner mints? Too often, it's the cigarette. And this time I'm serious.

So before your guests head outside for that after-dinner smoke (after all, you don't allow smoking in your home), let's talk lung health in a toxic environment.

An unhealthy diet isn't the only thing that can shorten our lives. Lung disease is the number-three killer in the United States, stealing away the lives of close to 361,000 Americans annually.

I used to smoke. Not a pack a day, but a pack a week, but, still, I have to wonder if, eventually, my lungs will suffer for my past indulgences, so, I asked my friend, Dr. Robert Daly, M.D., Medical Director of Respiratory Therapy Services of Community Hospitals Indianapolis, to explain what's really going on inside our lungs in a toxic environment. Here is the chest physician's fascinating response and sage life-saving advice:

Wendell, the lungs are your bodies "radiator." Just as in your car where the radiator takes the hot water and exchanges it for cool, the lungs take waste carbon dioxide and exchange it for oxygen. The bronchial tubes, like the radiator hose, deliver oxygen and carry off carbon dioxide. The business end of your lungs is the alveoli or the air sacks which act like vanes in the radiator to do the exchange work.

Now that you know the process in health, understanding

disease is easy. Chronic obstructive lung disease (COLD) is the most common lung problem. It's really two states. Chronic bronchitis is injury to the "hose," causing it to be twisted or kinked, slowing down the airflow. Emphysema is damage or loss of the air sacks (vanes of the radiator). This decreases the efficiency of the exchange. Asthma, on the other hand, causes the bronchial tubes to clamp down. It's like using too small a hose to deliver and remove water from the radiator.

The things that get you into trouble are also simple to understand. Tobacco smoke damages the bronchial tubes and air sacks causing COLD. So do hazardous mists such as air pollution (ozone and carbon monoxide) and hazardous chemicals at work or home. Work exposures include volatile organic compounds (benzene), solder flux, and caustics such as sulfuric acids. Home spray cleaners are notorious for causing irritation and spasm to the asthmatic patient.

Your best defense is to stop smoking. This simple act can add as much as five years of quality adjusted life no matter when you quit.

There now. Anybody want to help with the dishes?

CAN A VEGETARIAN AND A CARNIVORE LIVE IN THE SAME HOUSE?

Perhaps you and your housemates have different food tastes for your dinner each evening. Will it be necessary to go to battle? Who can forget the infamous scene in *Animal House,* when John Belushi, after squishing several bowls of Jell-O into his cavernous mouth, heaved the first cream puff in what has to become the most notorious food fight in cinema history. Sounds like fun, and don't tell me you never thought about having one.

Do you live in a mixed marriage? Is it "war and peas" or is it the "dawning of the age of asparagus"?

There are a variety of viewpoints, and if your household is like mine, nobody hesitates to express an opinion: "I don't like the taste of this"—"I'll get sick if I eat meat"—"Mommy, is this Bambi?"—"Ewww, I can't put a dead animal in my mouth!" Or, on the other hand: "Heck, my grandpa ate meat and bacon grease, and he lived to ninety-nine"—"Eating meat is bad karma"—"You gotta die from something, so shut up and pass the pork chops."

Having been a dedicated vegetarian over the last twelve years, I've heard it all, and have been exposed to frequent judgmental ridicule and scoffing. People fear and generally make fun of what they don't understand. When I first became a vegetarian, I weighed 265 pounds, about 90 heart-straining pounds overweight for my frame and body type. Eventually I lost all the excess weight and looked and felt better than I had in decades. But what was most frustrating was that instead of receiving flattering compliments from friends who hadn't seen me in a while, I got the impression that they were suspicious, as if something was mortally wrong with my health. Naturally, you have to factor in the equation that we live in a nation where over 50 percent of the population is overweight. Therefore, I stood out like the sore thumb they didn't want to deal with.

People just didn't get it, that being thin, healthy, glowing, and energetic was a normal result of consciously focused, balanced, vegetarian eating.

Sadly, I often heard hushed whispers behind my back: ". . . *buzz, buzz*, cancer? . . . *buzz, buzz*, AIDS?"

Gimme a break.

There's no doubt that a vegetarian diet, especially vegan, melts off pounds and inches when incorporated with regular aerobic exercise, but this is not the best reason for abstaining from meat.

I think it's the correct thing to do. Really, though, I'm willing to let you hamburger yourself into oblivion if that is your life's desire. I mean it.

Live and let live, that's the solution: acceptance. You, the vegetarian and you, the meat eater—you must realize that both must make loving concessions to achieve unity at the dinner table, and then, don't bug each other about it. Hopefully you have an understanding partner. I believe, however, in most cases of "mixed" couples, the meat eater changes more often.

I now offer the recipes for the meat-killing side of the family; the next chapter for the veggie murderers.

I don't understand why asking people to eat a well-balanced vegetarian diet is considered drastic, while it is medically conservative to cut people open and put them on cholesterol-lowering drugs for the rest of their lives.

— Dean Ornish, M.D.

Nonvegetarian Entrées

Chicken Dijonnaise

We've had this entrée on our catering menu for over 15 years and customers still request this satisfyingly rich chicken entrée. If you wish, use tempeh, pork, or seafood instead of chicken. Don't volunteer that the sour cream is nonfat and they won't know the difference.

4   boneless, skinless, chicken breast halves, cut into 1-inch pieces
1   pound of shiitake mushrooms
4   cloves of garlic, minced
1½ cups nonfat sour cream
3   tablespoons low-sodium soy sauce
¼   cup dry white wine
2   drops of liquid smoke
4   tablespoons Dijon mustard
    Black pepper to taste
1   pound whole-grain pasta, brown rice, or your favorite grain

Warm a nonstick skillet over medium-high heat, and then add the chicken. You don't need to add oil—the chicken will render enough fat to do the job. Why add fat to fat?

Sauté the chicken for 5 minutes to brown then add the mushrooms and the garlic. Reduce the fire to medium and stir frequently.

Add the white wine to deglaze the pan, scraping up the deliciously flavorful tidbits stuck on the bottom. Now add the soy, Dijon, sour cream, black pepper to taste, and liquid smoke. Mix well and simmer for 2 minutes.

Adjust seasonings and when ready to serve, place pasta or grain on a warmed dinner plate and top with the rich, creamy Dijon mixture. Serves 4.

Turkey Meatloaf

2   pounds ground turkey breast
2   egg whites
1   cup whole wheat bread crumbs
1   cup quick oats
$\frac{1}{4}$ teaspoon black pepper
1   cup chili sauce
3   tablespoons mushroom soy sauce or Kitchen Bouquet
1   cup each chopped onion, celery, and green bell pepper
1   cup skim milk or plain soymilk
1   tablespoon beef base

Preheat oven to 350 degrees.

Then simply mix all ingredients together in a large mixing bowl. Line a loaf pan with wax paper, fill with the meatloaf mixture, and bake on the center rack for 90 minutes or until the interior temperature has reached 180 degrees. (It is very important you are sure the loaf is thoroughly cooked to kill any bacteria present.) Serves 8.

Chicken with Apricot and Spices

4   boneless, skinless chicken breast halves
$1\frac{1}{2}$ tablespoons extra virgin olive oil
    Sea salt and black pepper
1   medium chopped onion
4   cloves of garlic, minced
$\frac{1}{4}$ teaspoon cinnamon

1   teaspoon cumin
1/2 cup chopped dried apricots
1   cup defatted chicken stock
2   tablespoons freshly squeezed lemon juice
1/2 cup apricot nectar
1/2 cup chopped fresh mint

Grab your chicken breasts and salt and pepper both sides. Warm the oil in a large nonstick skillet over medium-high heat, add the chicken and brown, about 3 minutes per side (the internal temperature should be 165 degrees). Remove chicken and keep warm.

Reduce the heat. In the same pan add the onion, garlic, cinnamon, cumin, and apricots and sauté for 2 minutes. Add the chicken stock, lemon juice, and apricot nectar, stirring to loosen the tidbits from the bottom of the skillet. That's where the yummy flavor is lurking. Cook for about 5 minutes, or until the sauce reduces and slightly thickens.

Return the chicken to the sauce and simmer for another 3–4 minutes. Adjust seasonings. To serve, top the chicken with the delicious apricot sauce then garnish with fresh mint. Serves 4.

Herbed Chicken, Potato, and Olive Salad

4   skinless chicken breast halves, cut up into bite-size morsels
1   teaspoon ground cumin
4   minced cloves of garlic, minced
1/4 chopped fresh habañero or 1 whole chopped jalapeño pepper
      (wear plastic food-service gloves or protect hands with
      plastic wrap when working with peppers)
    Sea salt and coarse-ground black pepper
1   red bell pepper, cut into thin strips
2   pounds new red or Yukon Gold potatoes, quartered
1/2 cup wheat germ
1   red onion, sliced onion-skin thin
1   cup black Greek olives, pitted and chopped
1/2 cup chopped fresh oregano leaves

½   cup fresh-squeezed orange juice
2   tablespoons extra virgin olive oil

Toss the chicken with cumin, garlic, and fresh chiles, and salt and pepper to taste. Place in a covered container or plastic zipper bag and marinate, refrigerated, at least 2 hours (overnight is even better).

Cook potatoes. Set aside and keep warm.

Roast the chicken at 375 degrees about 20 minutes, or to an internal temperature of 165 degrees. Toss the red bell pepper in with the chicken for the last 5 minutes of cooking time.

In a large mixing bowl, combine the potatoes with the wheat germ, red onion, olives, orange juice, and olive oil. Add the chicken and toss gently. (Flavors blend better while the food is still warm.) Serve immediately over a bed of mixed field greens along with some whole-grain bread and a glass of your favorite white wine. Serves 4.

Special note: When working with hot peppers, such as habañeros and jalapeños, protect your hands with plastic food-service gloves or plastic wrap. Getting all the pepper washed off your hands can be tricky, and if you touch your eyes—yow!

Asian Chicken

4   boneless, skinless chicken breast halves, cut into 1-inch strips
4   tablespoons lime juice
1   tablespoon minced garlic
    Spicy Hoisin Sauce (page 145)
    Toasted sesame seeds
2   scallions, chopped
    Fresh basil leaves

Marinate the chicken in lime juice and garlic for at least 2 hours.

Warm a nonstick sauté pan over medium-high heat. Add the chicken and cook 4 minutes, turning often.

In a mixing bowl combine the chicken with enough Spicy Hoisin Sauce to coat generously. Place on a wax paper-lined sheet pan and bake at

350 degrees for 5 minutes to glaze on the sauce. Garnish with toasted sesame seeds, chopped scallions, and fresh basil leaves. Serves 4.

Serving suggestions: Use the chicken to complete a slurpy lo mien dish. Serve along with your favorite grain or rice, a garden salad, and whole-grain bread for a family pleasing dinner. Or, leftovers can be used to make a sandwich the next day.

Steamed Fish with Lemon-Dill Sauce

The first time I steamed fish I fell in love with the simple process, which requires absolutely no oil or fat in the cooking process. The fish comes out so moist and tender you'll be amazed.

4	firm-fleshed fish fillets (Say that three times real fast!)
1/2	cup white wine
2	scallions
4	tablespoons Lemon-Dill Sauce (page 144)
	Fresh dill

Place a large steamer basket over a large pan of boiling water. Place the fish on a large dinner plate, pour the white wine over the fish, and place the scallions over the top. (If you don't have a steamer basket, improvise, but whatever vessel you use, be sure to apply a tight-fitting lid during the steaming process. Also, make certain that your plate will fit into the basket easily with an inch to spare around the edges— otherwise it will be extremely difficult to remove.)

Steam the fish for approximately 5 minutes or until the interior temperature reaches 165 degrees. (There we go with that temperature stuff again, but it is the best way to prevent under or overcooking and achieve perfection.)

Gently—and I do mean gently—remove the plate from the steamer. Reserve the fish and wine juices.

Arrange a bed of rice or cooked whole grain of your choice on a serving platter; place the fish on top, then pour the cooking juices over all.

Garnish with a dollop of Lemon-Dill Sauce, the scallions, and a few sprigs of fresh dill. Serves 4.

Special note: For an Asian twist, instead of wine, use a mixture of soy, ginger, mirin, and garlic when steaming the fish, and top with Green Tea Vinaigrette (page 68) instead of Lemon-Dill Sauce. Serve with some steamed baby bok choy for a truly far-Eastern flair.

Pork Tenderloin with Mustard Sauce

The success of this recipe lies with proper temperature control and the delicious sauce. Even though I don't eat animal flesh, the aroma of this dish drives everyone into a pork frenzy. As a vegetarian, however, I never trusted an animal that didn't sweat.

1   pork tenderloin (3 pounds)
3   tablespoons chopped garlic
      Sea salt and coarse-ground black pepper
¼   cup chopped onions
¼   cup minced shallots
½   cup dry white wine
2   tablespoons Dijon mustard
1   cup reconstituted nonfat dry milk

Massage the pork with the garlic and salt and pepper to taste. Place in a roasting pan and roast at 400 degrees for 20–25 minutes, or to an internal temperature of 165 degrees. Pull it out of oven and let rest for 5 minutes.

Meanwhile, in a saucepan combine the onions, shallots, and wine. Bring it to a boil, then reduce the heat and simmer for 3 minutes, or until reduced by one-half. Blend in mustard, milk, and salt and pepper to taste. Cook about 2 minutes longer, or till warmed through.

Slice the pork and serve, passing the sauce. Serves 8.

❧

CHAPTER EIGHT

How to be a Vegetarian —
Vegetarian Entrées

So now we get to the real meat—scratch that—the real *meaning* of the argument for strong nutrition. It's a call to change your life completely, to go vegetarian—from soup to nuts.

For a moment, let's get serious. So far I've gently urged you to make changes in your diet and lifestyle: to concentrate on fresh fruit and vegetables, preferably organic, restrict your use of meat, emphasize whole-grain products, drink wholesome water and exercise. I've include a chapter on delicious and nutritious meat dishes that I've used in my catering service.

Now I'm asking you to consider a radical change to help your suit on this earth—the only one you'll ever have.

My own experience and that of millions of others, especially recently, has provided irrefutable evidence that the best diet to maintain health is a vegetarian one.

Let's get down to basics and see, first of all, why vegetarian diet is a superior one for good health.

Following is a series of arguments, arranged in no particular order, which should convince a meat eater that he or she should take another look. (From *Diet for a New America* by John Robbins.)

The Environmental Argument

- Cause of global warming: greenhouse effect. Primary cause of greenhouse effect: carbon dioxide emissions from fossil fuels.

- Fossil fuels needed to produce a meat-centered diet vs. a meat-free diet: 50 times more.
- Percentage of U.S. topsoil lost to date: 75.
- Percentage of U.S. topsoil directly related to raising of livestock: 85.
- Number of acres of U.S. forest cleared for cropland to produce meat-centered diet: 260 million.
- Amount of meat U.S. imports annually from Costa Rica, El Salvador, Guatemala, Honduras, and Panama: 200 million pounds.
- Average per capita meat consumption in Costa Rica, El Salvador, Guatemala, Honduras, and Panama: less than eaten by average U.S. housecat.
- Area of tropical rainforest consumed in every quarter-pound hamburger: 55 square feet.
- Current rate of species extinction due to destruction of tropical rainforest for meat grazing and other uses: 1,000 per year.

The Cancer Argument
- Increased risk of breast cancer for women who eat meat 4 times a week vs. less than once a week—4 times.
- For women who eat eggs daily vs. less than once a week—3 times.
- Increased risk of ovarian cancer for women who eat eggs 3 or more times a week vs. less than once a week—3 times.
- Increased risk of prostate cancer for men who eat meat daily vs. sparingly or not at all—3.6 times.

The Natural Resources Argument
- Use of more than half of all water used for all purposes in the U.S.—livestock portion.
- Amount of water used in production of the average steer—sufficient to float a destroyer.
- Gallons to produce a pound of wheat—25.
- Gallons to produce a pound of meat—2,500.

- Cost of common hamburger if water used by meat industry was not subsidized by the U.S. taxpayer—35 dollars per pound.
- Current cost of pound of protein from beefsteak, if water was no longer subsidized—89 dollars.
- Years the world's known oil reserves would last if every human ate a meat-centered diet—13.
- Years the oil reserves would last if human beings no longer ate meat—260.
- Barrels of oil imported into U.S. daily—6 million to 8 million.
- Percentage of fossil fuel returned as food energy by most efficient factory farming of meat—34.5.
- Percentage of fossil fuel returned from least efficient plant food—32.8.
- Percentage of raw materials consumed by U.S. to produce present meat-centered diet—33.

The Cholesterol Argument
- Number of U.S. medical schools—226.
- Number requiring a course in nutrition—30.
- Nutrition training hours received by average U.S. physician during medical school—25.
- Most common cause of death in U.S.—heart attack.
- How frequently a heart attack kills in the U.S.—every 45 seconds.
- Average U.S. man's risk of death from heart attack—50 percent.
- Risk for average U.S. man who avoids the meat-centered diet—15 percent.

The Antibiotic Argument
- Percentage of U.S. antibiotics fed to livestock—55.
- Response of the European Economic Community to routine feeding of antibiotics to livestock—ban.
- Response of the U.S. meat and pharmaceutical industries to routine feeding of antibiotics to livestock—complete support.

The Pesticide Argument

- Percentage of pesticide residues in the U.S. diet supplied by grains—1.
- Percentage of pesticide residues in the U.S. diet supplied by fruits—4.
- Percentage of pesticide residues in the U.S. diet supplied by meat—55.
- Percentage of slaughtered animals inspected for residues of toxic chemicals including dioxin and DDT—less than 0.00004.

The Ethical Argument

- Number of animals killed for meat per hour in U.S.—500,000.
- Occupation with highest turnover rate in the U.S.—slaughterhouse worker.
- Occupation with highest rate of on-the-job injury in U.S.—slaughterhouse worker.
- Cost to render animal unconscious with captive bolt pistol before slaughter—$0.01.
- Reason given by meat industry for not using captive bolt pistol—too expensive.

The Survival Argument

- Athlete to win Ironman Triathlon more than twice—Dave Scott (6-time winner).
- Dietary choice of Dave Scott—vegetarian.
- Largest meat eater that ever lived—Tyrannosaurus Rex.
- Last sighting of Tyrannosaurus Rex—100,000,000 B.C.

And then there are these reasons . . .

- Number of people worldwide who will die of starvation this year: 60 million.
- Number of people who could be adequately fed with the grain saved if Americans reduced their intake of meat by 10 percent: 60 million.
- Human beings in America: 243 million.

- Number of people who could be fed with grain and soybeans now eaten by U.S. livestock: 1.3 billion.
- Percentage of corn grown in the U.S. eaten by people: 20.
- Percentage of corn grown in the U.S. eaten by livestock: 80.
- Percentage of oats grown in the U.S. eaten by livestock: 90.
- How frequently a child starves to death worldwide: every 2 seconds.
- Pounds of potatoes that can be grown on an acre: 20,000.
- Pounds of beef produced on an acre: 165.
- Percentage of U.S. farmland devoted to beef production: 56.
- Pounds of grain and soybeans needed to produce a pound of beef: 16.

God intended for the man and woman He had created to have dominion over all creatures. The Queen of England has dominion over all her subjects, but she doesn't eat them.

Let's assume that now you are at least halfway convinced. You'd like to take a baby—or maybe even a giant—step toward really eating right. Let's start with the main dishes on your table day by day.

Main dishes are at their best as vegetarian entrées. Give it a try. Go radical to eat right! To do that, you'll need to start with whole grains, which are the building blocks, the foundation of a healthy diet. *Amazing grains, how sweet the name . . .*

Whole grains are a source of energy. About 12,000 years ago, when agriculture was created, the majority of earth's inhabitants consumed a diet consisting of whole grains, whole-grain products, fruits and vegetables, beans, and minimal quantities of animal products—very much like the 2000-year-old Mediterranean/Bible diet.

After the technological advancements in agriculture in the 1800s, man's diet rapidly began to change. With the abundance of cheap grain, animal husbandry became profitable; therefore meat and dairy foods became more available and easy to purchase. With the invention of the roller mill, refining and grinding down vital grains, and separating the nutritious germ and bran portions from the endosperm,

SOME BENEFITS OF EATING WHOLE GRAINS

- Whole grains and plant foods can reduce the symptoms of chronic constipation, diverticular disease, and painful hemorrhoids.

- Whole grains are brimming with protective antioxidants and phytochemicals.

- Whole grains are a terrific source of cholesterol-lowering and cancer-fighting components.

- Whole grains are our body's main source of energy and fuel.

- Whole grains contain fiber, protein, carbohydrates, good fats, B complex, vitamin E, calcium, magnesium, potassium, manganese, iron, and copper.

- Whole grains are complete meals in themselves.

- Eating whole grains can lower cholesterol by promoting excretion of cholesterol through bowel movements.

- Whole grains take longer to digest, which allows more nutrients to be broken down and absorbed by the bloodstream.

- Whole grains can help regulate blood sugar by slowing down the conversion of complex carbohydrates into sugar. As a matter of fact, low-glycemic-index foods such as whole grains reduce hunger and can actually help to control weight, according to scientists at the USDA Human Nutrition Research Center at Tufts University.

the process of baking bread changed. Enter modern-day white bread with the 11 vitamins and minerals added.

Added? Where did those vitamins and minerals go in the first place? Unprocessed whole grains have three layers: bran, endosperm, and germ layers, but unfortunately, most grain products in America have been heavily refined to make them easier to cook. This is, of course, a nutritional wrong turn. The process of processing leads to the depletion of many vitamins, minerals, and other disease-fighting components.

The bran is the outer coating of the grain, and is loaded with fiber, B vitamins, and trace minerals such as copper and zinc. The germ, the part that would grow if the grain was sown, is also known as the embryo. It is a rich provider of vitamins E and B. After the bran and germ have been removed, all we have left over is the endosperm. The endosperm, a simple starch, is low in vitamins and fiber and is generally ground up for flour that would go toward producing overly processed foods such as white breads, pasta, pastries, and crackers.

When rice is likewise processed, and its outer coating and germ is removed—along with its nutrients—white rice is the result. Far preferable is brown rice, which is the staple grain of the vegetarian diet. Not only is it better for you, it tastes better.

But there are so many other exotic grains to which you need to be introduced. Millet is my favorite grain because of its alkaline properties. Packed with vitamins, copper, and iron, millet comes as small yellow balls, which far outdo whole wheat as a source of B vitamins. It can be made into a cereal, casseroles, and mashed (like potatoes). You can also add whole-wheat flour, egg whites, and diced vegetables, and fry millet as a patty—it's the only way I can get my wife to eat broccoli. I chop raw broccoli in the food processor until it's pretty well pulverized, then I combine it with the millet mixture, shape the patties, and sauté them in a little olive oil. (The sneaky chef strikes again.)

Quinoa (pronounced *keen-wa*), considered an ancient grain, is a protein powerhouse often referred to as the "super grain." Quinoa packs more iron than other grains and is a good source of many other

GRAIN COOKERY

Toasting really brings out the full flavor and texture of many whole grains. Place the rinsed and drained grain in a nonreactive skillet over medium-high heat and cook, stirring constantly until you smell a deliciously toasty aroma, about 5 minutes. When cooking, use a heavy pan with a tight-fitting cover.

		Ratio of Grain to Water	
GRAIN	COOKING TIME	GRAIN	WATER
Amaranth	20–25 minutes	1	3
Barley, pearled	35–45 minutes	1	3
Bulgur	20–25 minutes	1	2
Brown rice	45 minutes	1	2$\frac{1}{2}$
Cornmeal polenta	25 minutes	1	3
(stir constantly while cooking)			
Hominy grits	10–12 minutes	1	4
Kamut	2 hours	1	3
Kasha (buckwheat groats)	20–30 minutes	1	2
Millet	35–45 minutes	1	3
Oats, rolled	5 minutes	1	2$\frac{1}{2}$
Quinoa	20 minutes	1	2
Spelt (*soaked 60 minutes*)	30 minutes	1	3
Teff flakes	20 minutes	1	4
Triticale berries	15 minutes	1	2
Wheat, cracked	25 minutes	1	2$\frac{1}{2}$
Wild rice	60 minutes	1	3

Wendell's tips: *Be sure to keep the grain covered as it cooks to discourage scorching and evaporation of the cooking liquid. If you prefer, instead of water, use a vegetable or chicken stock for deeper flavor. Pressure cookers are the absolute best for cooking grains, but adjust cooking times according to directions with the cooker.*

nutrients like folate, zinc, niacin, thiamin, riboflavin, vitamin B6, magnesium, and phosphorous. Use it as you would rice.

Amaranth is the primary choice for persons who suffer from gluten intolerance. This grain is loaded with calcium, folate, and iron. It has a sweet but nutty flavor and is loaded with soluble fiber, which assists in lowering cholesterol.

Bulgur is whole-wheat kernels that have been cracked into different sized granules. You'll find it the main ingredient in tabbouleh salad.

Wheat berries are yet another name for whole-wheat kernels in their natural, unprocessed state. Wheat berries also add a wonderful texture to homemade wheat bread.

So, if you are one of those who think a balanced diet is a banana split in each hand, this information is just for you.

Beans figure next to grains as a protein-rich, main-dish food. Combine them with whole grains or brown rice and you have the food of life. Don't go against the grain—use your bean!

Forty years ago my mother frequently cooked up a tasty, belly-busting batch of ham and beans along with the obligatory cornbread. Thanks for the roughage, Mom.

She would patiently cook the beans, the poor man's meat, ever so slowly, all day, with a meaty morsel of ham and onions, combining to release an irresistible aroma that stimulated us into uncontrollable drooling and whining. Like the artful dodger, my older brothers and I would relentlessly beg her for a bowl of the delicious, hot mixture, accompanied, of course, by a large piece of cornbread with an inch-thick slab of butter on top. Remember those days? I'm still touting beans and cornbread, but not the ham and butter.

Did you know there are more than 14,000 specimens in the bean/legume family? However, only twenty-two are grown for human consumption. Those peanuts you snarf down at a basketball game are legumes, too.

Beans have been part of the world's diet since hunters and

gatherers roamed the earth, and are usually served along with a grain, which provides our earth suit with a perfect ratio of soluble and insoluble fiber. It is a perfect balance, the cornerstone of good health. Beans were consumed by the ancient Greeks who would hold an annual bean festival to honor Apollo.

By marrying beans and brown rice, you provide yourself with high-quality protein equal to that of meat and other animal sources. Beans or grains don't stand alone since their proteins are incomplete, or deficient in one or more of the essential amino acids. But beans and rice is a perfect marriage, and when you add the cornbread, it becomes even more complete, since corn is actually a grain, not a vegetable, as most of us assume.

A diet rich in bean fiber positively affects major health concerns of modern man, such as diabetes mellitus, heart disease, gastro-intestinal disease, obesity, hypertension, and cancer. The soluble fiber in beans is the same kind of gummy fiber found in oat products, which acts in the body to lower cholesterol and blood sugar. That's encouraging news for both diabetics and heart patients.

For most beans, one pound dried beans equal two cups uncooked, and 4–5 cups cooked. Cover and cook the beans thoroughly until they can be mashed with a fork. Check the water level frequently and add more when necessary.

Now let's suppose that after all that's been said so far, you're convinced. You want to try to make the "biggie" lifestyle change and become a vegetarian. Let's get really specific. How to make the jump? First let's get a couple of definitions straight:

What is a vegetarian?

Vegetarians do not eat meat, fish, or poultry—anything that had a mom or a face. Vegans, on the other hand, are vegetarians who abstain from eating or using any and all animal products, including eggs, milk, cheese, and other dairy items, wool, silk, and leather.

Most vegetarian diets provide less saturated and unsaturated fat, and fewer calories than typical nonvegetarian diets. They also have a higher content of fruits, vegetables, and whole-grain products.

The overall health of vegetarians might be better because most

INTERESTING BEAN FACTS

- Legumes are excellent sources of protein, especially when combined with grains. Beans are an excellent replacement for meat.
- The "woody," soluble fiber in beans can normalize bowel functions. Legumes with the highest amount of soluble fiber include lentils, pinto beans, and black beans. So, as you can see, all beans are *not* created equal.
- Soybeans are super-heroes, carefully guarding against the many maladies of aging. Research has strong data supporting the case for soy's role in preventing osteoporosis, cancer, kidney disease, and heart disease. Aim for at least 30 mg of isoflavones per day, but no more than 200 mg.
- Soybeans contain 8 essential amino acids necessary for human nutrition. Protein-rich soy contains about 7–13 g of protein per 4-ounce serving.
- Eating more soy could perhaps help stave off the irreversible brain disorder Alzheimer's disease, which affects more than half of Americans over the age of 85 according to a study presented at a meeting of the American Chemical Society in San Diego.
- If you are going to use canned or jarred beans, be sure to drain off all of the liquid and then rinse thoroughly to reduce salt and gumminess.
- The fiber content of beans slows the digestion of their carbohydrate content, regulating blood sugar levels. Finally, beans are very filling, which could force you to eat less and therefore lose a few pounds.

*Wendell's commandment: Thou shalt not weigh
more than thy refrigerator.*

༄

"Take thou also unto thee wheat, and barley, and beans, and lentils, and millet, and spelt, and put them in one vessel, and make thee bread thereof . . ."

—Ezekiel 4:9

Bread made from a combination of sprouted barley, millet, wheat, spelt, beans and lentils, can be found at most whole foods stores and bakeries. Ezekiel bread has been thoroughly analyzed and contains the full package of essentials for optimum health.

When David and his soldiers were fighting a war, David's allies brought them beans, grains, dairy products, and, more than likely, Ezekiel bread, to keep them fighting strong. According to the story, these allies brought

"earthen vessels, and wheat, and barley, and meal, and parched corn, and beans, and lentils, and parched pulse, and hone, and curd, and sheep, and cheese of kine, for David, and for the people that were with him, to eat; for they said: 'The people are hungry, and faint, and thirsty, in the wilderness.'"

—II Samuel 17:28, 29

vegetarians are health-conscious, exercise regularly, maintain a desirable body weight, and abstain from smoking, street drugs, and alcohol.

What are the health benefits of vegetarianism?

There is strong evidence that vegetarians have a lower risk of becoming alcoholic, constipated, or obese. They also have a lower rate of lung cancer.

The evidence is good that vegetarians have a lower risk of developing adult-onset diabetes, coronary heart disease, high blood pressure, and gallstones.

There also is some evidence that vegetarians have a decreased risk of breast and colon cancer, diverticular disease, kidney stone formation, osteoporosis, and tooth decay.

So, you've made the decision to become a vegetarian, but you scratch your head and mumble, "Now, where do I begin?" Well, the best place to start is to take an inventory of your pantry and refrigerator.

Our pantry at home is one of my favorite places. It is the heart of our kitchen, which is the heart of the home, and a pallet from which we can paint a canvas of beautiful, nourishing, and healing foods. It's a special place for my favorite foods, since, after all, I do all the cooking at home.

Vegetarianism crosses all ages, borders, and races, and, as you evolve, you will notice this eating lifestyle requires a wide variety of new and unfamiliar ingredients. But don't be discouraged. Look at it as an adventure. A well-stocked pantry can be your best friend.

Becoming a vegetarian is an evolution of sorts, as you slowly introduce your taste buds and your physiology to new foods. The effort must not be taken lightly. A person can't just wake up some morning and decide, "Hey, I think I'll become a vegetarian. All my friends are doing it." Our earth suit needs time to adjust to a new way of eating. If you've eaten meat all your life, your body has become

You are—and feel—what you eat

This is from my friend Heather Hedrick, vegan, triathlon winner, and nutritionist.

Wendell—

Every day is full of new adventures: work, family, social commitments, and physical activity. Most people would choose to tackle each day with a feeling of vigor and vitality. However, many people may not know that high levels of energy and spunk can be achieved, in part, through proper nutrition.

Each day we have the opportunity to choose how we will feed our bodies. Food is the fuel for our "machines" to be able to function in daily life and to participate in the activities we enjoy. If we do not supply our bodies with the proper fuel, our "machines" will become less efficient and effective. By choosing a well balanced, plant-based diet our bodies can function smoothly and we can maximize the potential of every day.

As a registered dietitian and triathlete, I have personally and professionally discovered how closely nutrition relates to physical performance. I recommend the following nutrition habits, repeated on a daily basis, in order to work toward physical excellence and optimal health:

Eat a plant-based diet. Choose less meat, especially red meat, and incorporate more beans, nuts, and soy products into your daily menus. Plant products are generally high in fiber, which helps to sustain energy during exercise and between meals, and low in total fat, preventing the lethargic feeling that often accompanies eating high fat meals.

Aim to consume three food groups in every meal. By creating balance in each meal, you will consume a variety of nutrients throughout the day. All nutrients are important in an active lifestyle to supply fuel for activity, replenish energy stores in muscles, and rebuild tissues.

Eat 5–10 servings of fruits and vegetables daily. Fruits and vegetables are packed with vitamins, minerals, and various phyto-chemicals that have a dramatically positive impact on our health.

Do not skip meals. Eat moderate amounts of food regularly throughout the day to keep energy levels high.

Monitor portion sizes at each meal and snack. By eating until satisfied, versus feeling stuffed and uncomfortable, we can allow our bodies to stay energetic throughout the day. Large amounts of food require our bodies to slow down in order to digest properly.

Stay hydrated every day. Drink a minimum of eight to twelve cups of water per day. Carry a water bottle with you at all times and sip it continuously throughout the day.

We are what we repeatedly do. Excellence, then, is not an act, but a habit.

—Aristotle

accustomed to digesting meat, but when you quit meat, your body needs a sufficient amount of time to readjust itself to less animal fat and new clean plant proteins. In addition, you also need to read at length on the subject, educate yourself, and make a serious lifelong commitment to a new lifestyle, which will catapult you into an entirely new level of wellness. Becoming vegetarian is not simple. Much knowledge is needed to insure you get the proper nutrition and balance. Foregoing meat means giving up on certain essential vitamins, minerals, and nutrients, especially the B vitamins. As a rule, all vegetarians should supplement with a sublingual liquid solution B complex with folic acid and a plant-based multivitamin.

Once my wife, Sandi, and I committed to vegetarianism, our meat consumption was gradually reduced from five times a week to two times, to one time, and then none. However, we noticed toward the end of our meat-eating days, when we did cheat and savor those last few morsels of meat, we would become ill, green with nausea, and our stomachs felt like we swallowed a rock. It was nature's way of telling us something was wrong. The physical evolution had begun. No more hard-to-digest, partially decomposed animal protein. Our bodies were giving us a message. Indigestion and heartburn were soon something of the past.

One beautiful fall weekend, Sandi and I decided to go the hills of Brown County, Indiana, for the weekend. Traditionally, we begin our weekend outings with a lovely meal at our favorite local eatery and this weekend was no exception. We waltzed in, found an empty table, perused the menu and decided, "What the heck, it's vacation—let's cheat." We proceeded to order hamburgers and onion rings. They were delicious.

Full and satisfied, we waddled out to our car and drove off into the hills to our cabin nestled in the ear-shattering peace and quiet of southern Indiana. But all the beauty on earth couldn't have saved us from our fate. We both spent the first day of our retreat in fetal position, trying to get comfortable and escape the steely fingers of nausea that swept through our GI tracts. A half bottle of Pepto and a package of Rolaids later, and we were somewhat back to normal. That memorable day in Brown County turned out to be the final time we consumed meat or fried foods, with nary a regret.

LET'S HAVE A PANTRY RAID

Be patient. Altering your pantry to fit the needs of a vegetarian diet will take some time, an open mind, education, and experimentation.

First, empty your pantry shelves and wash them with a mild bleach solution. Then, while they dry, proceed with the following:

Check all cooking oils to ensure they aren't rancid, and toss out any oils or shortenings that are hydrogenated. Stock cooking oils such as olive oil, peanut oil, and other unhydrogenated vegetable oils. Toss the canola and shortening! (They call it shortening because it shortens your life.)

Check expiration dates on everything. At the same time, let's be practical, there's no sense in throwing everything out, so try to use as much as you can and not be wasteful. Slowly replace items as they run out until your entire pantry is "safe."

Then add these staples: Whole grains such as wheat berries, amaranth, brown rice, quinoa, millet, bulgur, spelt, soy, and barley. During hot weather, keep grains in the freezer for a longer shelf life. Oils have a tendency to go rancid rapidly at room temperature. Also stock organic beans, dried, bottled, or canned.

Add to your shopping list unbleached organic all-purpose flour, organic whole-wheat flour, whole wheat bread, baking soda, aluminum-free baking powder, Sucanat (**Su**gar-**Ca**ne-**Nat**ural), crystallized sugar, cane juice, Stevia, honey, maple syrup, brown rice syrup or barley syrup, blackstrap molasses, unsulfured molasses, sea salt, nutritional yeast flakes, nonstick spray for cooking and baking, vinegar (red wine, rice wine, balsamic), kombu strips, wasabi powder, and nori sheets (for sushi). Also, whole-grain pasta, Japanese soba buckwheat noodles, and instant ramen noodles; pasta sauce, madras curry powder, and low-fat coconut milk. Cans of tomato paste, canned organic vegetables (drain and rinse off the briny juice before eating), canned organic soups, canned organic tomatoes and tomato paste, vegetable stock, soy nut butter, whole-grain crackers (read the label!), baked tortilla chips, rice cakes, jarred salsa, roasted red peppers, natural peanut butter (Smuckers makes a natural peanut butter that advertises "no trans-fats"), and dried herbs (herbs over six months old have lost their oomph and should be discarded and replaced with freshly dried or purchased herbs).

Also, cinnamon, chili powder, cumin, black pepper, mustard, five-spice powder, onion powder, garlic powder, allspice, nutmeg, bay leaf, sage, rosemary, tarragon, vanilla extract (or any other of your favorites), fresh organic garlic, organic onions and potatoes, and assorted dried chile peppers. Goodies would include walnuts, pecans, pine nuts, cashews, organic coffee, sugar-free hot cocoa mix (watch out for mixes that contain hydrogenated oil), Raja's Cup (a delicious antioxidant coffee substitute), organic green tea, sesame seeds, toasted sesame oil, soy sauce, mushroom soy sauce, plum paste, tahini paste, dried fruits (sulfur-free, such as raisins, prunes, figs, apricots, dates, cranberries, or apples), dried shiitake mushrooms, nonfat powdered milk, nonfat evaporated canned milk, organic granola and other whole-grain cereals, organic soy milk, carob chips, oatmeal and grits, no-sugar-added jelly, and wheat germ.

Refrigerated staples should include soymilk (I suggest vanilla), distilled drinking water, soy cheese slices, low-fat soft and hard cheeses, individually quick-frozen (IQF) vegetables (keep several varieties on hand) such as spinach, broccoli, cauliflower, brussels sprouts, peas, and other varieties that please you.

Other items to keep in the fridge include soy bacon, organic milk, flax oil, tempeh, tahini, miso, flax seed for grinding (an Omega-3 bonanza), low-fat mayonnaise, good-quality Dijon mustard, organic tofu in varying degrees of firmness, nonfat sour cream and nonfat cream cheese, salad dressing, organic yogurt, active dry yeast, fruit-sweetened apple butter, sauerkraut, olives, pickles, capers, fresh herbs (such as rosemary, basil, cilantro), Parmesan cheese or tofu imitation Parmesan cheese, a variety of fresh seasonal fruits and vegetables, frozen entrées, organic fruit juices, fresh ginger, liquid smoke, good red and white wines for cooking (and red wine for drinking—one glass per day to receive benefits).

Nonedibles should include unbleached coffee filters, paper towels, and paper napkins; a gallon of bleach for sanitizing cutting boards and food preparation areas to prevent cross contamination and food poisoning; a battery-powered transistor radio, a flashlight, candles and some matches; extra batteries, blankets, a first-aid kit, an alternative heating source, and a fire extinguisher.

Establish par levels to ensure you won't run out of anything important in the event of an emergency power failure or a national disaster. It could be a life-saving strategy to use your pantry as a survivor back-up tool, especially if it contains a back-up of your important prescribed medications. Also, keep a propane burner handy with extra gas cartridges. You just never know, but I'll go along with the old adage: "Chance favors a prepared mind," or, in this case, a properly prepared pantry.

I am not a vegetarian because I love animals: I am a vegetarian because I hate plants.

— A. Whitney Brown

You put a baby in a crib with an apple and a rabbit. If it eats the rabbit and plays with the apple, I'll buy you a new car.

— Harvey Diamond

Vegetarian Entrées

Honey Whole Wheat and Millet Bread

Absolutely nothing compares to the pride one feels as he removes his first loaf of intoxicatingly aromatic bread from the oven. It's almost ceremonial. Baking bread has taught me a valuable lesson in life—patience. Each batch of bread can be different, due to various factors: your mood, the air temperature, the humidity or lack thereof, or lack of focus during the kneading procedure. Wait for the rubber bands of gluten to appear and you'll have it nailed every time. You can't speed it up or slow it down, so be patient and go with the flow.

- $1^{1}/_{4}$ cups warm water (110 degrees F)
- 3 tablespoons honey
- 1 package ($^{1}/_{4}$ ounce), or $2^{1}/_{4}$ teaspoons active dry yeast
  Pinch of sea salt
- $1^{1}/_{2}$ cups organic whole-wheat flour
- 2 cups organic unbleached bread flour
- $1^{1}/_{2}$ tablespoons vital wheat gluten
- $^{1}/_{4}$ cup chopped walnuts
- $^{1}/_{8}$ cup washed and rinsed millet
- $^{1}/_{8}$ cup sesame seeds
- 3 tablespoons organic unsweetened applesauce

Prepare a sponge, or yeast starter for the bread, by pouring the warm water into a medium-size mixing bowl and adding 1 tablespoon of honey and the yeast. With a whisk, gently stir thoroughly to eliminate clumps.

Cover and set in a warm area (but no more than 85 degrees or you're courting disaster) until the mixture is frothy and double in size.

Combine the dry ingredients in a large mixing bowl. Add the applesauce, yeast mixture, and the remaining 2 tablespoons of honey. Mix well with a sturdy wooden spoon or your freshly washed hands.

Now comes the fun part. Clear off a work area and dust it with flour. Remove the bread mix from the bowl and slap it down on the worktable and begin to knead. Knead for at least 15 minutes.

Place the bread in a large, oiled bowl and cover with a damp towel. Set in a warm, draft-free area (about 75 degrees) and let rise for 1 hour, or until double in size. Punch dough down and turn it over; cover again with the damp towel and let rise for another 35 minutes or until it has again doubled. Be sure to not place the rising bread too close to a heat source or it won't rise, due to the untimely death of the yeast.

Meanwhile, oil a 9x5-inch loaf pan. Punch the dough down, shape it, and then place it into the prepared bread pan. Cover with your damp towel and in a warm spot for about 30 minutes or until double in size. (This makes a total of three times this bread has risen.)

Bake at 350 degrees for 35–45 minutes or until the interior temperature of the bread has reached 200 degrees. Remove the aromatic bread immediately from the bread pan and cool on a rack so the bottom of the bread will not get soggy. Makes a 1–1$\frac{3}{4}$-pound loaf.

Special Note: This fiber-rich bread freezes beautifully. It's great for PBJ or SoyBJ sandwiches, or you can make a grilled cheese using soy cheese, served with a hot, steamy cup of organic tomato soup.

Special note: If you lack the time or the patience to put this loaf together, bring out and dust off the bread machine. Place ingredients in the bread machine pan in the order suggested by the manufacturer. Select the proper dough cycle and begin.

Sweet Amaranth Quick Bread
(Wheat-free)

6   cups organic amaranth flour
1   tablespoon aluminum-free baking powder
9   cups brown rice
4   teaspoons sea salt
3   egg whites, lightly beaten (optional)
1   cup soymilk, rice milk, or water
6   tablespoons honey
2   tablespoons vegetable oil

Lightly oil two 9x5-inch loaf pans and dust with a bit of amaranth flour.

Sift the amaranth flour and baking powder together. Combine with the remaining dry ingredients.

Combine the liquid ingredients in a large mixing bowl. With a wooden spoon, gradually stir in the dry ingredients. Stir just enough to be sure all ingredients are well blended, but do not overmix.

Arrange the oven rack to the center and heat oven to 350 degrees. Divide the batter equally between the two loaf pans and bake for 45 minutes or until a tester comes out clean when inserted at the center.

Allow the bread to cool completely in the pans. If you attempt to remove this wheat-free bread from the pan while warm it will crumble. Serve immediately or wrap tightly and freeze.

Special note: Using either soy or rice milk instead of water will impart a deeper, richer flavor to this dense bread. Plus, using these milks will add more important disease-preventing phytonutrients and vitamins.

Toasted Corn and Quinoa

1   tablespoon extra virgin olive oil
2   cups fresh or frozen corn
1/2   teaspoon cumin
1/2   teaspoon chili powder
1   small onion, chopped

 1 clove garlic, chopped
    Sea salt and pepper
 2 cups cooked quinoa
 1 tablespoon chopped fresh cilantro for garnish
    Fresh lime juice

Warm a nonstick skillet over medium heat and add the olive oil and corn. Cook till the corn begins to become golden and caramelized.

Add the spices, onion, garlic, and salt and pepper to taste. Stir, adjust heat to low, and gently sauté for 3–4 minutes.

Add the quinoa and stir thoroughly till heated through. Serve garnished with chopped cilantro and a squeeze of fresh lime.

Tofu Parmesan

 ¼ cup wheat germ
 ¼ cup cornstarch
 1 container organic firm silken tofu
 2 tablespoons olive oil
 1 pound of your favorite whole-grain pasta
    Sea salt and pepper
 2 tablespoons Parmesan cheese or tofu Parmesan
 2 tablespoons low-fat mozzarella cheese or soy mozzarella
 1 10-ounce jar marinara sauce
 2 tablespoons chopped basil leaves

Combine the wheat germ and cornstarch. Drain the tofu and thoroughly blot with paper toweling to remove excess moisture. Slice the blob in half horizontally and dredge with the wheat germ and cornstarch mixture. Set aside.

Add the oil to a nonstick sauté pan and warm over medium heat. Sauté the tofu for about 7–8 minutes per side, or until it is golden brown and beginning to firm up. This long cooking will give the tofu a more mouth-pleasing consistency. Turn the tofu pieces only once, as too much handling will break it up. Be patient and gentle with your spatula.

Meanwhile, cook the pasta. Drain and rinse; set aside and keep warm.

Place the sautéed tofu on a wax paper-lined baking sheet. Sprinkle with salt and pepper to taste. Top with the Parmesan and mozzarella cheeses and spoon a generous portion of marinara over the cheeses. Bake at 350 degrees for 5 minutes or until the cheeses melt. Serve over a bed of the pasta. Add more marinara and cheese as desired, and top with fresh basil. Serves 2.

Special note: This recipe works well with chicken too. It's always nice to offer some hot pepper flakes with this dish. A caesar salad and some crusty whole-grain bread would round it out perfectly.

Asian Whole-Grain Stir-Fry

This all happens rather quickly, so have all the ingredients ready and lined up before you begin. I strongly urge you to use a large nonstick sauté pan for this dish. You'll have better results.

	Soy sauce to taste
1	tablespoon tahini
3	tablespoons peanut oil
1	piece fresh ginger (1 inch), peeled and minced
3	tablespoons minced garlic
1	white onion, diced
1	red bell pepper, diced
1	cup broccoli florets
1	carrot, unpeeled, diced
2	cups cooked pinto, soy, or white beans, drained and rinsed
1	cup frozen peas
1	pinch crushed red pepper (optional)
4	cups cooked brown rice, quinoa, millet, or barley
6	scallions, chopped
¼	cup toasted nuts (your favorite)

In a small bowl, whisk the soy sauce and the tahini together.

Warm the peanut oil in a nonstick sauté pan over medium heat. Add the ginger, garlic, and onion and cook till translucent, about 2 minutes.

Next add the red bell pepper, broccoli, and carrot, and stir-fry for 2 minutes. Now add the beans and stir them into the mix.

Turn the heat to low and add the tahini-soy mixture and peas. Add the crushed red pepper if desired. Cook 1 minute, or until all ingredients are heated through.

Serve on a bed of the cooked rice or other grain, and top with the chopped scallions and toasted nuts. Serve with a slice of whole-grain bread, a vegetable salad, and pride. Serves 6.

Wendell's tip: Ginger is easier to mince if you smash it with the broad side of a chef's knife before you begin to chop.

Fried Tofu with Enchilada Sauce, Diced Vegetables, and Millet

1   container organic firm silken tofu
4   tablespoons extra virgin olive oil
1   teaspoon chopped garlic
1   carrot, unpeeled, diced
2   stalks of celery, diced
1   green bell pepper, diced
1   can enchilada sauce
1   jalapeno pepper, seeded and chopped fine
1   splash of hot sauce
1   tablespoon chili powder
6   cups cooked millet
6   tablespoons of chopped fresh cilantro

Drain the tofu and thoroughly blot with paper toweling. Slice the tofu horizontally, then into 1-inch cubes.

Warm the oil in a nonstick skillet over medium-high heat. Add the tofu cubes. Cook, stirring frequently—and gently!—until all sides are nicely browned, about 10 minutes. Be patient.

Reduce heat to medium and add the garlic, carrot, celery, and green bell pepper. Sauté for 2 minutes. Add the enchilada sauce and simmer for 2 minutes.

Spoon millet onto warmed dinner plates. Make a well in the center and fill with the tofu mixture. Garnish with chopped fresh cilantro. Serves 6.

Fakin' Bakin' Vegetable Stir-Fry

Fakin' Bakin' is made by Light Life Products and can be found at many grocery and whole foods stores. This satisfying entrée is brimming with soluble and insoluble fiber, minerals, complex carbohydrates, monounsaturated fats, phytonutrients, phytoestrogen, vitamins E, B, C, protein, and beta-carotene. Whew!

4	tablespoons extra virgin olive oil
3	cloves of garlic, minced
1	teaspoon cayenne pepper
4	strips of Fakin' Bakin', cooked and diced
3	cups of assorted diced vegetables: carrots, red peppers, cauliflower, broccoli, scallion, peas, zucchini, or celery
½	cup vegetable stock or defatted chicken stock
1	cup black soy beans, well drained and rinsed (or any bean of your choice)
½	cup pitted and chopped Kalamata olives
¼	cup tomato sauce
4	cups cooked brown rice
	Fresh cilantro, chopped

Warm the olive oil in a nonreactive sauté pan over medium-high heat. Add the garlic, cayenne pepper, and Fakin' Bakin'. Sauté, stirring frequently, about 2 minutes. Don't walk away.

Add the vegetables and sauté for another 2 minutes, stirring constantly. Pour in the stock, beans, olives, and tomato sauce. Reduce heat to low and simmer for 2 minutes. Remove the pan from the heat.

Mold servings of rice by pressing into a 1-cup measuring cup or dish. Turn the molded rice onto warmed dinner plates and spoon the stir-fry mixture around the rice. Garnish with cilantro. Serves 4.

Blackened Cajun Tempeh Steaks in Creole Sauce

1   package multigrain organic tempeh
    Cajun Spice Rub (page 147)
3   tablespoons extra virgin olive oil
1/2 cup each of diced celery, carrots, green bell pepper, and onions
1/4 cup Jack Daniels Sour Mash or other whiskey
2   tablespoons Dijon mustard
1/2 cup vegetable stock
1   tablespoon tomato paste
    Splash of hot sauce
    Salt and pepper to taste

Cut the tempeh into three equal portions. Coat lightly with nonstick spray and generously dredge with the Cajun Spice Rub. Wrap the tempeh and let it marinate for at least 1 hour.

Warm the olive oil in a nonstick skillet over medium heat and add the marinated tempeh. Sauté for about 5 minutes. Add the diced vegetables and cook for another 5 minutes, or until the tempeh is browned.

When tempeh is golden brown, add the whiskey (stand back if you're using an open flame) to deglaze the pan. When the alcohol has burnt off, add the Dijon, stock, tomato paste, and hot sauce and salt and pepper to taste. Simmer briefly for 2–3 minutes. Adjust seasonings. Serve over whole grains alongside a crispy, fresh, vegetable salad. Serves 4.

Hoosier Rice Patties

Ever since the senior George Bush announced to the entire nation that he "hated broccoli," it's been a tough sell for that wonderful vegetable, especially for my wife. She used to love it, but lately has lost her taste for the cruciferous vegetable. This is one of the few ways I can get her to eat broccoli, since you can't really taste it—but the cancer protection is still there. You have to be lovingly sneaky sometimes.

2   stalks fresh broccoli

4 cups cooked brown rice
1 medium chopped onion
3 egg whites or ¾ cup liquid egg substitute
2 cups organic whole-wheat flour
½ cup chopped parsley
1 tablespoon sea salt
1 teaspoon black pepper
   Extra virgin olive oil
½ cup grated Parmesan cheese
   Fresh chopped parsley

Peel the broccoli stems, and coarsely chop stems and florets. Place in a food processor and process until it's almost pulverized. Combine the broccoli and the remaining ingredients in a large mixing bowl and mix well with your hands. Cover and refrigerate for at least 1 hour.

Warm a nonstick skillet over medium heat and pour in just enough olive oil to coat the bottom of the pan. Spoon a small bit of the mixture into the hot skillet and shape it with the back of a spoon. Cook it, then test it. Is the seasoning all right? Is it firm or does it break up? If it's too thin and doesn't hold together, add a touch more flour. If it's too heavy, add a bit of water or veggie stock.

Spoon the mixture into the oiled skillet and shape into circular ½-inch-thick patties. Avoid having the patties touching each other. Sauté until cooked through and golden, about 7–8 minutes per side, turning only once. Adjust heat as necessary to avoid burning. (Note: The more you fiddle with them, the more apt they are to break up. When the sides have begun to firm up, it's time to turn.) Dust with Parmesan cheese and parsley. Serves 8–10.

Serving suggestion: The cooked patties can also be topped with low-fat mozzarella and marinara sauce; bake them for 5 minutes at 350 degrees, or until the cheese melts, then serve over a bed of pasta.

Vegan Wheat Berry Veggie Casserole

1 butternut squash, peeled and cubed, to make 2 cups

1   cup sliced unpeeled carrots
1   cup sliced yellow squash
2   cups cooked wheat berries
2   tablespoons chopped scallions
1/2 cup chopped parsley
1   tablespoon low-sodium soy sauce or shoyu
2   cups shredded tofu cheese
    Cracked black pepper

Place the butternut squash and carrots in a steamer basket and steam for 10 minutes or until tender. (They can also be microwaved in a dish covered with a very damp towel.)

Combine the veggies, wheat berries, scallions, parsley, and soy sauce or shoyu in a 2-quart casserole. Sprinkle with cheese and broil for 5 minutes or until the cheese has melted and browned slightly. Serves 4.

Boraccho Beans

1   tablespoon extra virgin olive oil
1   medium onion, chopped
1   medium unpeeled carrot, diced
1   medium red bell pepper, diced
2   canned chipotle peppers, chopped, or 1 can (4 ounces) of
        chopped green chiles
4   cloves garlic, minced
1   can (15 ounces) each of pinto and kidney beans, drained and
        rinsed
1   cup strong beer
1/2 cup chopped black or green olives
2   teaspoons cumin
1/2 teaspoon coarse-ground black pepper
1   cup grated low-fat cheddar cheese or soy cheddar cheese
2   tablespoons snipped fresh cilantro for garnish

Warm the olive oil in a large saucepan over medium-high heat. Add the onion, carrot, red bell pepper, chipotle peppers or chiles, and garlic. Cook briefly and do not overcook—there still needs to be a little crunch left in the vegetables so all of the valuable nutrients are not destroyed.

Stir in the beans, beer, olives, cumin, and black pepper. Gently bring the mixture to a soft simmer over medium-high heat and cook for about 2 minutes, stirring occasionally.

Pour beans into a warmed serving bowl. Sprinkle with cheese and cilantro. Keep a bottle of hot sauce on the table for those brave souls who believe, "Mo hotter is mo better." Serves 4–6.

SAUCES AND GRAVIES

Mushroom Gravy

Usually gravy is an artery-clogging fat food as a result of its animal-based components. This gravy, however, has very little fat and tastes great on just about anything, especially Smashed Potatoes.

4	tablespoons extra virgin olive oil
1	onion, finely chopped
1	medium unpeeled carrot, grated
1	celery stalk, minced
1	bay leaf
2	cups thinly sliced mushrooms (stems, too)
6	cups vegetable stock
1	can tomato paste
1/4	cup mushroom soy sauce
1	cup red wine
	Cornstarch

In a nonreactive stockpot, warm the oil over medium-high heat. Add the onion, carrot, celery, bay leaf, and mushrooms. Sauté for 3 minutes.

Add the vegetable stock, tomato paste, mushroom soy, and wine. Bring to a boil and cook for 5 minutes.

Meanwhile, prepare a cornstarch slurry by mixing equal parts cornstarch and water. Mix well with a fork or small whisk. (Or put the cornstarch and water in a lidded jar and shake.) Add the slurry to the simmering liquid a little at a time to thicken. Whisk constantly at first, then use a wooden spoon to reach the corners of the pot. Add more slurry as desired, until gravy reaches desired thickness. Serve immediately, or cool and refrigerate.

Special note: Ground up flax seeds also make an excellent thickening agent for sauces, gravies, and soups (as well as making good breadings and coatings). Use your (clean) coffee grinder to pulverize these Omega-3-rich flax seeds. Arrowroot, on the other hand, makes a lousy gravy-thickening agent, and some people find the texture offensive. Try agar instead.

Lemon-Dill Sauce

This sauce is great for raw vegetables, baked potatoes, served over fish, or as a sandwich condiment.

1   cup nonfat mayonnaise
1   cup nonfat sour cream
1/4 cup minced fresh dill
2   tablespoons minced fresh parsley
    A squeeze of fresh lemon juice or vitamin C crystals
1   teaspooon minced fresh garlic
1   minced scallion
    Sea salt and pepper to taste

Combine all ingredients and refrigerate overnight. Makes 2 1/2 cups.

Sweet and Pungent Sauce

1   inch of fresh ginger, peeled and minced
1   cup rice vinegar
1   cup Sucanat or 1/2 cup of Stevia powder
3   tablespoons cornstarch
1/2 cup water
1 1/2 cups pineapple juice

¼ cup orange juice concentrate
2 tablespoons low-sodium soy sauce
1 tablespoon vitamin C crystals

In a food processor, combine the ginger, vinegar, and Sucanat or Stevia. Process until the ginger somewhat disappears. (The mixture will darken from the Sucanat.) Make a slurry by combining the cornstarch and water and mixing well.

Combine the pineapple juice and orange juice concentrate in a nonreactive saucepan. Place over medium-high heat and bring to a boil. Add the ginger-vinegar mixture, soy, and vitamin C crystals. Bring to a boil again and stir in the cornstarch slurry. Cook, stirring, until mixture thickens. If it becomes too thick, add a bit more fruit juice.

Special note: This sauce is great with egg rolls, grilled chicken or fish, or as an ingredient for a sour cream-based vegetable dip. Experiment with other fruit juices for more exotic flavors and colors.

Spicy Hoisin Sauce

1 head of garlic, peeled and minced
2 inches of fresh ginger, peeled and minced
1 jar hoisin sauce
1 cup toasted sesame oil
⅛ cup Thai pepper flakes
1 tablespoon powdered star anise
2 cups shoyu or soy sauce
1 teaspoon fish sauce (optional)
2 tablespoons freshly squeezed lime juice

Process the garlic and ginger in a food processor till fine. Add the rest of the ingredients and blend until all are incorporated. Thin with more soy sauce if necessary.

Special note: Adding a little unsweetened coconut milk (low-fat, of course) will turn this sauce into a big flavor monster. Use this sauce on chicken or beef satay as a dipping sauce, or as a glaze for tempeh, grilled chicken, pork, fish, or shrimp.

Mirin Sauce

A great glaze for baked tofu, tempeh, chicken, or fish.

1/2   cup low sodium soy sauce or shoyu
1/2   cup mirin (sweet sake)
      Juice of one large orange
1/2   cup defatted chicken stock or vegetable stock
2   tablespoons honey
1   inch of fresh ginger root, peeled and minced
2   cloves of garlic, minced
1   pod of star anise, split
1   tablespoon cornstarch
1   tablespoon water

In a saucepan, combine soy sauce, mirin, orange juice, stock, honey, ginger, garlic, and anise. Over medium-high heat, bring to a boil.

Mix the cornstarch with the water to make a slurry and gently stir it into the boiling mixture. Reduce heat to medium-low and simmer until the sauce thickens and becomes shiny. Remove anise. Makes 1 1/4 cups.

Maple Mustard Sauce

Forget the tempeh or fish! This sauce is so good you'll want to eat it with a spoon.

1/2   cup soy sauce
1/4   cup toasted sesame oil
1/4   cup real maple syrup
1/2   cup Dijon mustard
1   teaspoon toasted Szechwan peppercorns

Whisk all ingredients together and store in an enclosed container in the refrigerator. This all-purpose sauce can be used as a glaze for tempeh, fish, chicken, vegetables, tofu, or as a dip for raw vegetables.

∿

Cajun Spice Rub

Your can massage this on tempeh, fish, chicken, pork loin, or shrimp, and by marinating you create a full-flavored entrée. Marinate overnight for the best results. This is the same mix used to blacken fish or chicken. If it's too hot, back off on the cayenne pepper. Shooe-wee!

1/4	cup kosher salt
1/8	teaspoon cayenne pepper
1/4	cup paprika
1/4	cup granulated garlic
4	tablespoons onion powder
2	tablespoons dried thyme
2	tablespoons white pepper
2	tablespoons allspice
2	tablespoons dry mustard

Combine all ingredients and store in an air-tight container.

Special note: If you mix this seasoning mix with sour cream, Dijon mustard, a wee splash of Jack Daniels, and some chopped scallion, you'll end up with an outstanding dip for vegetables or a baked potato topping. You could also use this creamy sauce as a decadent topping for your completed blackened entrée.

Caribbean Pepper Wine

Congested? You won't be after you savor this vibrantly spicy tropical marinade. Hot peppers are nature's best decongestant, a tasty way to find relief.

4	cups medium-dry sherry
1	tablespoon crushed red pepper or 1 habañero pepper, seeded and minced fine (wear gloves for this, or protect your hands with plastic wrap)
1	teaspoon allspice

1/2 teaspoon dried thyme leaves
1/4 cup orange juice concentrate
1 tablespoon cracked black pepper
    Pinch of sea salt

Combine everything in a saucepan and simmer over low heat for 5 minutes. Store in the refrigerator.

Lo Mein Sauce

4 tablespoons cornstarch
1 cup water
2 tablespoons toasted sesame seed oil
1 tablespoon fresh minced ginger
1 tablespoon fresh minced garlic
1/2 teaspoon crushed red pepper
1 teaspoon five-spice powder
1 cup soy sauce
1/3 cup mirin (sweet sake)
3 tablespoons honey

Dissolve the cornstarch with the water.

In a saucepan, combine the toasted sesame oil, ginger, garlic, crushed red pepper, and five-spice powder. Simmer over medium-low heat for 1 minute. Add the soy sauce, mirin, and honey. Increase heat to medium-high and bring the mixture to a boil. Mix the cornstarch with the water and add to the boiling sauce. Continue cooking until mixture thickens. (It should be just slightly thickened, not gravy-like.) Cool, then store covered in the refrigerator.

Special note: Use this sauce combined with noodles, protein (such as tofu or tempeh), diced veggies, scallion, and chopped cilantro for an outstanding Asian lo mein. Add toasted sesame seeds for more nutrition and texture. Also, you can marinate tempeh, chicken, pork, or seafood in this multipurpose sauce for a deep, rich flavor.

CHAPTER NINE

Desserts and Treats

Let's lick the sugar blues! A teaspoon of sugar, by any other name, is still a teaspoon full of sugar, and our entire nation is literally high on sugary sweetener. It's reaching epidemic, overdose levels!

Contrary to what we may have been taught to believe, sugar is addictive, a lucrative, legal drug thought of as benign because of its perceived innocence, socialization potential, and aggressive marketing capacity. And after all, it is what little girls are made of.

A look at labels or at articles in hundreds of periodicals and books reveals that everything Americans drink—soft drinks, coffee, milk, beer, tea, juices, distilled spirits, and wine, is loaded with sugar or artificial sugars.

For many people, eating sugar-rich foods creates an appetite-rebound effect. Sugary foods spike the level of glucose in their blood, thus causing the body to release a rush of insulin, the hormone responsible for absorbing glucose into muscle, liver, and fat cells. When the "high" subsides in a few hours, a biochemical depression can occur. This depression leaves these people with a feeling of extreme hunger, which can only be satisfied by eating more sugary foods, thus an endless cycle that is nutritiously unhealthy and may promote obesity.

The average American adult consumes close to two hundred pounds of the white stuff and approximately sixty-two gallons of "liquid sugar" (AKA soft drinks) annually. To visualize that amount, picture forty-five one-pound bags of sugar sitting on your counter at home. Of course, that includes the sugar that is hidden in processed junk foods, making the grocery store shelves moan with their mass. If you are looking for a growth market investment during these times of market volatility, and don't care about socially responsible investing, consider the sugar and soft drink industry.

The Center for Science in the Public Interest states that "liquid candy" has outpaced every other beverage, with per capita consumption of soft drinks by Americans doubling in the last quarter century, increasing by 43 percent since 1985.

The consumption of bottled water, beer, and milk, doesn't come near to the mind-boggling 62 gallons of empty-calorie, nutrient-robbing soft drinks chugged down annually. Burp! The average American consumes 25 percent of his or her calories from some form of refined sugar, according to Nancy Appleton, Ph.D., in her book, *Lick the Sugar Habit*.

I haven't mentioned the delicious, calcium-leaching, no-calorie phosphates that come absolutely free in each can. Oh, my, another reason to worry about the snap, crackle, and pop of osteoporosis.

Researchers have found that when we eat sugar, we increase the rate at which we excrete calcium, which makes bones brittle, and chromium, a vital mineral, which helps maintain stable blood sugar levels. Need I say more? Yes.

In *The Sugar Blues*, William Dufty states: "Science has discovered that sugar taken every day leaves our bodies in a perpetual acid condition. In an attempt to rectify the situation more minerals are required from deep in the body to correct the imbalance. Finally, in order to protect the blood, so much calcium is taken from the bones and teeth that decay and general weakening begin."

Several years ago I met a woman who casually shared with me that her sister had recently had a baby who was born with more than fifty broken bones. I asked her if she liked sugar and she said, "Oh yes, I love sugar. I use it in all my recipes at home; actually, my whole family is fond of sugar." Case closed. Book 'em, Danno.

Remember when we used to put copper pennies in a can of Coke and in three days they would be totally dissolved? Boy, how cool. Imagine what it does to our GI tract. Even back in 1951, a doctor who had been in charge of nutritional research for the U.S. Navy during World War II testified before a congressional committee about the consumption of Coca-Cola, said that he was "amazed to learn that the beverage contained substantial amounts of phosphoric acid." They put human teeth in a cola beverage and found "they softened and started to dissolve within a short period of time." The sugar content masks the acidity.

Coca-Cola, which sells over a billion soft drinks daily, stated in a recent corporate report, "We're just getting started."

One new marketing strategy currently in place is to encourage having Coke or Mountain Dew as a breakfast drink as an accompaniment to a sugary breakfast pastry. In other studies, researchers found a positive correlation between processed sugar overconsumption and eight forms of cancer: colon, rectum, breast, ovary, prostate, kidney, nervous system, and pancreas. In some cases, the risk was more than doubled by consuming sugar on a regular basis. (E. M. Hass, *The Detox Diet*, 1996.)

Although we don't need refined or excessive amounts of sugar, we *do* need some sugar. That spoonful of sweet stuff that helps the medicine go down is the main source of energy for your brain and muscles. You need to assure that sufficient sugars are consumed, because glucose is essential in the composing of serotonin, "the happy-maker."

All sugars are not created equal, nor are aspartame, or Nutrasweet, maple syrup, high-fructose corn syrup (the worst), or honey. Check out the label on a bottle of Aunt Jemima's pancake syrup.

Processing sugar or sugar beets purges the white stuff of virtually all of its nutrients, thus the term, "empty calories." On the other hand, Sucanat, sugar from the first squeezing, still has a plethora of minerals and nutrients.

Sucanat can be found at any whole foods store, and with it you won't have to worry about the rebound effect. Practice moderation. Other options are Stevia and brown rice syrup. Stevia (recently under fire and controversial itself) comes from the leaf of a plant indigenous to Peru.

I can only conclude that you should avoid aspartame like the plague. Here is an excerpt from *Anti-Constitutional Activities and Abuse of Police Power By the U.S. Food and Drug Administration and Other Federal Agencies* by James Demeo, Ph.D., Director of Research at the Oregon Biophysical Research Laboratory.

> The FDA has received over 5,500 complaints against aspartame (Nutrasweet), which was legalized amid controversy regarding the capacity of this substance to alter brain hormone balances; some 9 percent of the complaints today involve serious neurological effects, including seizures.
>
> A recent major study by UCLA researchers of 109 patent-drug advertisements found eighty-one to be "inaccurate, misleading, and even dangerous."

In another book, *Aspartame (NutraSweet): Is It Safe?*, H. J. Roberts, M.D., states "The truth about aspartame's toxicity is far different than what the NutraSweet Company would have your readers believe. In February of 1994, the U.S. Department of Health and Human Services released the listings of adverse reactions reported to the FDA (DHHS 1094). Aspartame accounted to more than seventy-five of all adverse reactions reported to the FDA's Adverse Reaction Monitoring System (ARMS). Some reactions to aspartame were very serious, including seizures and death. Other reactions reported included headaches/migraines, dizziness, joint pain, nausea, numbness, muscle spasms, weight gain, rashes, depression, fatigue, irritability, tachycardia, insomnia, vision loss, hearing loss, heart palpitations, breathing difficulties, anxiety attacks, slurred speech, memory loss, loss of taste, and vertigo."

It sounds like the many of the symptoms of fibromyalgia or chronic fatigue syndrome, doesn't it?

Armed with this information we must make changes and become role models for our children and especially our grandchildren, our most precious possessions. Children continue to grow and need quality nutrients to grow in health until they are at least nineteen years of age. Otherwise diseases that affect Americans at fifty to sixty years of age will strike them earlier in life, perhaps in their twenties and thirties. Diabetes is already at an epidemic level due to poor nutrition and sloth.

It would seem, after reading this information, ironic, that at every holiday or birthday celebration of life, we eat food that ultimately will make us ill and possibly kill us. Every piece of cake our grandchildren eat with us is filled with sugar and food coloring, which profoundly affects our physical and mental health and our ability to fight off disease, flus, colds, and ear infections. It is very painful to watch my grandchildren eat so much refined sugar, but TV advertisements and peer pressure can be very persuasive.

Try these books for good reading: The *I Can't Believe This Has No Sugar Cookbook* by Deborah E. Buhr, and *The Sugar Blues*, cited above, by William Dufty

Having said all this about sugar and sugar substitutes, we must still face the facts: Worldwide, people love sweet-tasting desserts. From way back, when inn cooks in Sumerian times (3,000 B.C) fixed honey cakes and Roman kitchen slaves slaved over fruit ices and fig tarts, people have loved to finish supper or dinner with dessert. Here, I offer you some scrumptuous meal-finishers that won't finish you permanently.

Sweets 'n' Treats

Oatmeal Raisin Cookies

Everyone loves cookies, and this recipe won't let you down, plus, these cookies are loaded with health enhancing vitamins, minerals and fiber. Remember, allow your sweets craving guests to enjoy your dessert first, then let them know it was healthy. The jaws will drop.

COMBINE:

1	cup unsweetened organic applesauce
2	cups Sucanat
1	cup liquid egg substitute
1	teaspoon vanilla

Mix well by hand or with a mixer. Set aside.

COMBINE:

1	cup organic unbleached white flour
1	cup organic whole-wheat flour
1/2	cup wheat germ
1	teaspoon aluminum-free baking powder
1	teaspoon baking soda
2 1/2	cups organic instant oats
1/2	teaspoon sea salt
1/2	cup carob chips
3	cups organic raisins (sulfur-free)

ADD THE DRY INGREDIENTS TO THE WET INGREDIENTS AND MIX WELL, THEN FOLD IN:

1   cup of your favorite nuts or seeds: walnuts, almonds, sunflower seeds, cashews, or hazel nuts (or a blend for a wider variety of nutrients)

Preheat oven to 350 degrees. Line a baking sheet with parchment paper and drop portions of the cookie mixture onto the baking sheet.

Place the tray on the middle rack of the oven and bake for 10 minutes. Rotate the pan 180 degrees and bake 1–2 minutes longer. The cookie should be moist and chewy. Let them cool before you shovel them into your anxiously awaiting mouth. Makes about 36 cookies.

Special note: I've always had success portioning out cookies with a 2-ounce ice cream scooper. Occasionally dip the scoop into some warm water to keep the cookie dough coming out easily.

Special tip: Your grocery stores now carry a relatively decent nonfat or low-fat cream cheese. If you really want to be naughty, try spreading some of it on one of these delicious cookies for a real treat. People often comment that it tastes like a Little Debbie's Oatmeal Pie.

Pumpkin Chocolate Muffins with Cream Cheese Centers

All right, you've been good 90 percent of the time and now you're ready to be a little bad. These delicious muffins my wife invented, with the treat inside, are real crowd pleasers, plus, the health benefits of pumpkin are well documented, so chow down, enjoy, and lose the guilt. This does not mean, however, that you can devour 6 of these muffins at one sitting. If sugar gives you a hangover, eat a bowl of millet to undo the acidic damage.

We use butter in this recipe which, I personally feel, is the lesser of two evils when it comes to baking. Margarine has more problems attached to it than butter.

1²/₃ cups unbleached organic all-purpose flour
 ¹/₂ cup sugar

$^1/_2$ cup Sucanat
$^1/_2$ teaspoon cinnamon
 1 teaspoon nutmeg
$^1/_2$ teaspoon allspice
$^1/_2$ teaspoon mace
 1 teaspoon baking soda
$^1/_4$ teaspoon aluminum-free baking powder
$^1/_4$ teaspoon sea salt
 2 large eggs or $^1/_2$ cup liquid egg substitute
 1 cup canned pumpkin
$^1/_2$ cup melted butter
 1 cup chocolate chips or carob chips
$^1/_2$ cup chopped walnuts
    Low-fat cream cheese

Lightly coat a muffin pan with nonstick spray.

Mix the flour, sugar, Sucanat, spices, baking soda, baking powder, and salt in a large bowl.

In another bowl, combine the eggs or egg substitute, pumpkin, butter, nuts, and chocolate or carob chips and mix until blended.

Add the egg and pumpkin mixture to the dry ingredients. Fold all ingredients together with a rubber spatula until well-moistened. Do not overmix.

Fill the muffin cups half full. Add a teaspoon of cream cheese to the center of each muffin, and then cover with more batter until the cups are three-fourths full—but no more than that.

Bake at 350 degrees for 20–25 minutes or until puffed and springy when touched in the center. Cool muffins for about 10 minutes, then remove from the pan. Makes 8 large or 12 medium muffins.

ॐ

Tofu Pound Cake

Your guests will not be able to tell the difference!

 2 cups unbleached white cake flour
 4 teaspoons aluminum-free baking powder
1¹/₂ teaspoons sea salt
 1 pound organic soft silken tofu
³/₄ cup real maple syrup or honey
 1 teaspoon vanilla extract
³/₄ teaspoon almond or orange extract

Lightly coat a 9x5-inch loaf pan with nonstick spray and dust lightly with flour.

Sift together the flour, baking powder, and salt.

In a food processor, combine the tofu, maple syrup or honey, vanilla, and almond or orange extract. Process until smooth.

Add the tofu mixture to the dry ingredients and mix just until well-combined. Do not overmix.

Bake at 350 degrees for 30–35 minutes or until golden brown and the top springs to the touch. If the cake begins to get too brown, tent some foil over the top.

Remove the cake from the pan and let cool slightly on a wire rack. To prevent a hard crust from forming, while the cake is still a little warm, wrap it tightly first in wax paper and then foil. Serves 12.

Crème Brulée

    Sucanat for dusting
 4 tablespoons cornstarch
 1 tablespoon vanilla extract
1¹/₂ cups nonfat sweetened condensed milk
7¹/₂ cups skim milk or reconstituted nonfat dry milk
 3 cups liquid egg substitute
³/₄ cup Sucanat

Spray 12 ramekins with nonstick spray and dust with Sucanat.

Dissolve the cornstarch in the vanilla extract and some of the milk. Make sure there are no lumps.

In a large mixing bowl, combine the cornstarch mixture, condensed and skim milks, and liquid egg substitute. Aggressively whisk the mixture. Then gently and carefully, divide the mixture evenly among the ramekins.

Place the filled ramekins in a 9x13-inch baking pan. Pour boiling water into the baking pan SLOWLY, being extra careful to not splash any water into the ramekins. The water should come about $2/3$ to $3/4$ up the sides of the ramekins. Err on the side of caution—if water gets into the mix, it will not become a custard. Bake at 350 degrees for 40–50 minutes or until a toothpick inserted in the center comes out clean. Watch it carefully—overbaking will cause the custard to break down and become weepy. (And so will you.)

Cool on a wire rack, then cover and chill for at least 2 hours.

To serve: Preheat the broiler. Place the custards on a sheet pan and sprinkle the $3/4$ cup of Sucanat evenly over the tops, about 1 tablespoon per ramekin. Place in the oven on the middle rack and broil until the Sucanat has melted and begun to turn a caramelly brown, about 4–8 minutes. Do *not* walk away from the oven unless you want to court disaster! Top with a few red raspberries and serve immediately.

Blueberry Almond Coffee Cake

(Recipe courtesy of Deb McClure-Smith)

1	cup unbleached white flour
$1/2$	cup Sucanat or sugar of choice
$3/4$	teaspoon aluminum-free baking powder
$1/4$	teaspoon baking soda
$1/2$	teaspoon sea salt
$1^1/2$	cups fresh blueberries, divided use
$2/3$	cup low-fat buttermilk

2 tablespoons butter, melted
1 teaspoon vanilla extract
¼ teaspoon almond extract
1 large egg
¼ cup sliced almonds
1 tablespoon Sucanat
¼ teaspoon cinnamon

In a large bowl, combine the flour, Sucanat or sugar, baking powder, baking soda, and salt. Stir in 1 cup of blueberries.

Combine buttermilk, butter, vanilla and almond extracts, and egg in a bowl. Whisk to blend.

Coat an 8-inch pan with nonstick spray. Spoon in batter and spread evenly. Top with the remaining blueberries.

Combine almonds, 1 tablespoon of Sucanat, and cinnamon and sprinkle over the top. Bake at 350 degrees for 35 minutes or until toothpick inserted in center comes out clean. Serves 8.

Special note: For best results, when measuring flour, lightly spoon it into a measuring cup and level it off by scraping a knife across the top.

New World Rice Pudding

1 cup brandy or rum
1 cup raisins
7½ cups soymilk or skim milk
1 teaspoon vanilla extract
½ teaspoon cinnamon
1 tablespoon lemon zest
½ cup wheat germ
⅔ cup basmati or jasmine rice, washed and rinsed
⅔ cup of Sucanat or ½ cup Stevia powder

Warm the rum or brandy and add the raisins. Let set for 30 minutes, then drain the raisins. Reserve the liquid.

Lightly coat a 3-quart, nonreactive baking dish with nonstick spray.

Combine the milk, vanilla, cinnamon, lemon zest, wheat germ, rice, and raisins and pour carefully into the baking dish.

Bake covered at 375 degrees for 45 minutes. Stir in the Sucanat or Stevia and bake 10–15 minutes longer. (If pudding seems a little dry, add a bit more milk.) Let cool, then chill, uncovered, for at least 2 hours. Serves 6.

Special note: The rice in this rich dish could be easily replaced with brown rice, however, the rice must be cooked first.

Moist Vegan Brownies

12 ounces organic soft silken tofu
$^2/_3$ cup water
$1^1/_2$ cups plus 6 tablespoons unbleached all-purpose flour
$1^1/_2$ cups Sucanat or brown sugar
1 teaspoon sea salt
1 teaspoon vanilla
1 cup toasted pecans or walnut pieces
$^3/_4$ cup unsweetened cocoa
$^1/_2$ cup unhydrogenated vegetable oil
1 teaspoon aluminum-free baking powder

Coat a 9-inch square baking pan with nonstick spray and dust with flour. Don't forget the corners.

Purée the tofu in a food processor.

Grab a saucepan and add the water, 6 tablespoons of flour, and puréed tofu. Cook over low heat, stirring frequently with a wooden spoon, until heated through and through, about 2–3 minutes.

Transfer the mixture to a mixing bowl and allow it to cool. Mix in the Sucanat or sugar, salt, vanilla, and nuts and blend well.

In another bowl, combine the cocoa and oil. Add the remaining $1^1/_2$ cups of flour and the baking powder. Now take that mixture and, still using your wooden spoon, blend in the cooled-down tofu mixture. Do not overmix.

Scrape the mixture into the prepared baking pan. Bake at 350 degrees for 25 minutes or until the top is dry and springs back when lightly pressed. Please, allow them to cool down before you began whacking away at these invitingly aromatic delights; otherwise they'll break apart and become crumbly. (You can just wait a minute, okay?) Makes 24 brownies.

Ambrosia

1   cup chopped walnut pieces
2   bananas, sliced
1   11-ounce can mandarin oranges, drained
1   cup fresh diced pineapple (canned won't work as well)
1   cup vanilla organic yogurt
¼   cup nonfat sour cream
1   cup shredded coconut
2   tablespoons orange juice concentrate

Place the nuts in a small skillet over medium heat. Lightly toast the nuts until you begin to notice the wonderfully nutty aroma. Stay near the pan, don't walk away. It takes only about 3 minutes.

In a nonreactive mixing bowl, combine the orange segments, banana, and pineapple.

Add the remaining ingredients, and let flavors marry for a few hours in the refrigerator. Serves 6.

English Trifle

What a delicious and healthy way to celebrate the Fourth of July with this beautifully assembled, cold dessert. Make it up ahead of time and refrigerate for a cool treat on a hot day.

1   angel food cake
¼   to ½ cup Chambord (or other raspberry liqueur)
½   pint each of strawberries, blueberries, and raspberries
1   cup vanilla organic yogurt

1   cup nonfat sour cream
1   bunch of fresh mint

Combine the yogurt and sour cream in a mixing bowl.

Slice the cake. In a clear glass or crystal serving bowl, arrange $1/3$ of the cake slices. Drizzle with the liqueur. Top the cake with $1/3$ of the fruit, then $1/3$ of the yogurt and sour cream mixture.

Repeat the layering process 2 more times. Top with a sprig of fresh mint and present to oohs and aahs. Serves 4.

Special note: Try using peaches and peach liqueur for another flavor explosion.

Basic Vanilla Tofu Cream

This deliciously deceiving dish is the vegetarian's version of a crème anglaise. Make the sauce thicker or thinner based on your tastes. It will complement your desserts with its sweet, rich flavor and consistency. Try it on a warm vegan brownie.

1   pound organic soft silken tofu
2   tablespoons unhydrogenated vegetable oil
$1/2$ teaspoon sea salt
1   tablespoon vanilla extract
2   tablespoons fresh squeezed lemon juice
2   tablespoons real maple syrup

Place all ingredients together in a food processor and process till smooth and creamy. Store refrigerated. Serves 8.

Special note: Add a tablespoon or two of a fresh juice concentrate for a fruit sauce to spoon over fresh fruit salad. Use it as a topping for angel food cake or Moist Vegan Brownies (page 160).

If you want it to have a little yellowy-egg tint (like the real McCoy), add just an itsy-bitsy pinch of turmeric. Omit the syrup and vanilla to turn the sauce into a bechamel. Or, add Parmesan cheese and a pinch of nutmeg, and you have alfredo sauce.

Raspberry Dream Pie

2 cups natural graham cracker crumbs
1/2 cup wheat germ
1/4 cup chopped pecans
1/4 cup unhydrogenated safflower oil
4 cups fresh raspberries
2 tablespoons lemon juice
1 cup organic soft silken tofu
1/2 cup rice syrup or real maple syrup
1 teaspoon vanilla

Combine graham cracker crumbs, wheat germ, pecans, and oil; mix well and press into a glass pie plate. Bake at 350 degrees for 10 minutes. Let cool.

While crust is baking, combine raspberries with lemon juice. Set aside.

Combine tofu, syrup, and vanilla in a food processor, and purée until smooth. Add to the raspberries and and stir until well-blended. Spoon into the crust.

Bake at 350 degrees for 7 minutes or until the berries are soft and juicy. Remove from the oven and cool thoroughly in refrigerator to set. Garnish with additional berries and serve cold. Serves 6–8.

BREAKFAST TREATS

French Toast

How often can you eat a delicious breakfast and get your daily portion of protein and disease-preventing isoflavonoids simultaneously?

8 ounces organic soft silken tofu
4 teaspoons Sucanat or 2 teaspoons Stevia powder
3/4 cup vanilla soymilk

1   teaspoon vanilla extract
¼   teaspoon sea salt
½   teaspoon cinnamon
6   ½-inch-thick slices whole-wheat bread
2   tablespoons vegetable oil

Drain the tofu and blot with paper toweling to remove excess moisture. In a food processor, combine the tofu, Sucanat or Stevia, soymilk, vanilla, salt, and cinnamon. Purée at least 2 minutes, scraping down the sides of the bowl occasionally, until mixture is smooth.

Pour the mixture into a large bowl. Dip each piece of bread into the liquid several times to coat each side. Leave the bread in the mixture to relax for several minutes so the liquid gets totally absorbed.

Lightly coat a nonstick skillet with a bit of the vegetable oil and warm over medium-high heat. When the pan is hot, add the soaked bread and cook about 2 minutes on each side or until golden brown. This is the time you have to be flexible—adjust the heat if the toast is browning too quickly or too slowly. Pay attention.

Serve immediately with real maple syrup, not a high-fructose corn syrup, maple-flavored version. Serves 6.

Serving suggestions: Offer a variety of fruit toppings to ease the craving for butter. This high-protein, deliciously custardy treat can also be served as a dessert.

Oatmeal Pancakes

For successful pancakes, be sure to mix the dry ingredients separately from the wet, and then mix them together. Over-beating will ruin the outcome; lumps are okey-dokey. Make the batter six hours in advance or preferably, the night before, for perfect flapjacks every time. This is slow food, not fast food.

Combine:
½   cup unbleached all purpose flour
1   teaspoon aluminum-free baking powder

Combine:

1   egg or ¼ cup liquid egg substitute
½   cup nonfat evaporated milk
¼   cup water
4   teaspoons Sucanat or 2 teaspoons Stevia powder
2   tablespoons unhydrogenated vegetable oil (or, if you absolutely must, melted butter)

Combine the wet ingredients with the dry ingredients and stir in:

1½   cups of cooked oatmeal

Preheat the griddle over medium-high heat. (Test the griddle with a few drops of the water. If they dance and bead up, the griddle is ready.)

Dip ¼-cup portions of batter onto the anxiously awaiting griddle and when the cakes bubble at the edges, flip them and continue cooking until they are golden brown. Adjust heat as necessary. Makes 12 pancakes.

CHAPTER TEN

Lighter Fare —
In the Trenches, or,
Beyond the Kitchen Doors

Without the slightest hesitancy, I acknowledge that the brightest, most enjoyable years of my young culinary life were spent slinging hash on the East Coast in kosher delis, flirting with customers, learning how to cook juicy briskets, curing fatty pastrami, peeling tongue, slicing exorbitantly expensive sides of lox and sturgeon, rendering cholesterol-laden schmaltz, slicing mounds of warm bagels and red corned beef, and puréeing buttery, ubiquitous, artery-clogging chopped liver.

It was a unique experience for a young, naive WASP Hoosier boy to learn from the kind, gentle, older Jewish deli men. I can still recall the aromas that assaulted my senses as I entered a delicatessen: the garlic from the pickles, the smell of freshly cooked meats, the plump knockwurst, and the aroma of homemade chicken soup with delicate matzo balls. And I must not forget gefilte fish with the obligatory, deep, beet-red horseradish and piles of shiny, fragrant challah, the braided Sabbath bread. By and large, kosher cooking is a respected, healthy, chemical-free and clean way of eating, wrapped up in many centuries of tradition and dietary laws.

Not much can compare with a properly cooked, thinly sliced corned beef brisket sandwich on dark rye bread with Swiss cheese, mustard, and cole slaw right on the sandwich, served with a kosher pickle and a crispy potato latke on the side. Although this sort of food is incredibly tasty, it's also unbelievably calorie-laden, loaded with chicken fat or schmaltz, nitrates and nitrites, fatty meats, MSG, unhealthy oils, and sodium. So practice moderation—something I didn't learn to do in my counter-culture years.

The Deli Haus in Kenmore Square, Boston

Like school, a job is a way to learn life's valuable lessons, both good and bad. Working in a variety of restaurants and bars through many years taught me some of the finer things in life, and also some of the wackiest, wildest, most bizarre, and often life-threatening ones.

Working behind the scenes in these high-energy, stress-filled, fast-paced restaurants offered me a perfect environment for learning about human nature. There's nothing cerebral involved in making a career out of being a line cook, salad prep, waiting tables, being a captain, or busing dirty tables, and most people have to think about something while they carry loads of plates slopping off spaghetti sauce, as they wait to get a better job. A typical restaurant employee's thoughts center on sex, drugs, alcohol, money, and rock 'n' roll. Momma, don't let your children grow up to be line cooks. It's only a job, rarely a future.

At the end of the shift, the staff usually partied by chemically altering their consciousness, hanging out in bars, spending hard-earned tips, listening to loud psychedelic music, and then, hopefully hooking up. Everyone's attractive at 2 A.M.

In retrospect, I feel nauseated and ashamed for wasting hard-earned money promoting the wholesale destruction of brain cells, not to mention my liver.

During the 1967 Summer of Love, the Deli Haus in Boston's Kenmore Square was owned and micromanaged by my soon-to-be mentor, "Whitey." There was plenty of free food, a decent paycheck, willing college women, laughs, and also great opportunity to learn a craft. Grease was in my blood.

The "Smelly" Haus, as we called it, was one of those typical Boston restaurants down a few stairs off the sidewalk on Commonwealth Avenue with classic deli food. There were old-time wall-hanging jukeboxes positioned at every booth, lots of mirrors for depth, and a bevy of aging, surly waitresses who had been there for ten years and knew every customer by name. The air was perfumed with the smell of garlic pickles.

"Come on, men, get those orders out quicker! You should all be truck drivers! Let's go! Let's go!" Whitey would bellow during the busiest, most stressful time. We'd freak out when we looked up and saw the never-ending line waiting to be fed.

On occasion, Pearl Fox, my favorite waitress, would get my attention and then we'd meet in the walk-in refrigerator, close the door behind us and relieve our stress by screaming. The practice of primal therapy had worked beautifully every time, except once when Whitey happened into the kitchen, heard the commotion coming from the walk-in, and opened the door. We stopped in mid-scream, frozen like raccoons in the headlights. He gave us a wide-eyed look of astonishment, turned around and walked away mumbling and shaking his head in disbelief.

Mistakes were not tolerated, and if we couldn't keep up with the orders, Whitey would loudly nag us in front of the customers and shame us into better performance. As a food service owner, I can attest there is an entirely different work ethic, or lack thereof, in the U.S. today than when we worked our hearts out then.

Whitey and I soon bonded and he would take me out on his thirty-eight-foot yacht every Saturday and Sunday. Up until then, I had observed the ocean, but never ventured out on it. Sundays, accompanied by his family, we would proceed to catch a bushel full of flounder, which would ultimately become Monday's lunch special at the Deli Haus. Good profit, and great fun for a wide-eyed Billy-Bob from landlocked Indiana. I think Whitey befriended me simply because he felt sorry for this naive, fundamentalist Hoosier boy plucked fresh from the cornfields. You could easily have compared me to Woody from the TV show *Cheers*—likeable but inexperienced, not in the least bit aware.

At the Deli Haus, after the crew set up their stations, we would sit back and wait for the big rush. Near the hand-gravity slicer, and directly next to the boiling steam table, I vividly recall the "hash bucket": Every end and scrap of brisket, corned beef, knockwurst, roast beef, or pastrami was to be saved during the eight-hour shift, and at the end of the day the seething, festering bucket-o'-meat was then used to make beef hash for the breakfast rush.

Any meats were game, no matter how long they'd been sitting at the perfect bacteria breeding temperature: below 140 degrees and above 41 degrees. It's a wonder we didn't kill anyone, since, back in the seventies, we knew precious little about the dangers of salmonella, *E. coli*, and bacterial cross-contamination. Quite frankly, we took few or no precautions to protect our customers from food-borne illness. One could easily buy a good health inspection report with a C-note and a bottle of Jack Daniels. Not so, today, thankfully. Local board of health inspectors are much more conscientious and concerned about food-borne illness than they were thirty years ago.

We were required to pour copious amounts of sodium bisulfate on "questionable" meats and foods to preserve their shelf life. You could turn visually unappealing, rusty lettuce into a perfect-looking salad mix just by soaking (bleaching) in an unhealthy chemical solution. Most restaurateurs were simply and blissfully unaware of the connection between food and sickness, and then if someone did get sick, it was blamed on a stomach bug. The symptoms are similar.

Today, standards to control food-borne bacterial infections are set by Hazardous Analysis Critical Control Point (HACCP), a program set up by NASA and Pillsbury to protect the astronauts from food-borne illness while in space. In addition, every airline catering company across the U.S. must follow HACCP standards and go through rigorous testing in order to gain approval. Because our catering company services major airline carriers and charters, we also are required to abide by the same stringent standards.

I chuckle as I'm reminded of an unforgettable customer who frequented the Deli Haus every morning for his usual breakfast of hash and eggs. Steve was the "Norm" of the Deli Haus, an average-looking, lonely, albeit likable, single Jewish gentleman in his mid-twenties. He had jet-black hair and a dramatic, involuntary head twitch to the right.

Steve was a needy kind of guy who thrived off the attention that the familiarity and warmth of a local neighborhood delicatessen could offer a loyal, regular customer. He'd stroll through the door, everyone would yell out "Hi Steve!" and before his posterior hit the stool he would give Mary his order: "I think the hash sounds good today."

"Hey, Steve, you want an egg with that?" the line cook grunted.

"Why not? But don't cook it too long—I like them runny." A real double whammy due to the possibility of bacterial contamination from the hash and an invitation to salmonella from undercooked eggs.

The physical layout of the Deli Haus was an early version of the currently popular "open kitchen" concept. At that place, everyone in the dining room could watch his food being prepared, which made it most difficult for the line cooks to get away with any unsavory behavior, such as dropping your meal on the floor. Ask those in the business and they will tell you that more food drops on the floor than the public wants to know. No line cook wants to recook an order and get yelled at by the manager for wasting food, or by a tip-hungry waitress stressing out on the timing of the meal.

As you may recall, I mentioned earlier that working in restaurants could be hazardous to your health. Let me share a few incidents to illustrate the point:

After the Deli Haus days, I went to Copley Square to work at The Bulkie, a well-regarded delicatessen run by the legendary David Zide, another talented, demanding, hard-driving perfectionist. It was a big deal back then for me to get the nod from the boss to go into the kitchen and make some cold salads like vinegar cole slaw, tzimmes, creamy macaroni salad, and mustard potato salad. It got me off the line dealing with the stress of demanding customers. Perhaps I wasn't always too careful.

One day Dave called me into his office. As I entered, trembling with apprehension, he invited me to sit down and I couldn't help but notice he was twisting a ring around his pinky finger. "Mendel (Mendel was my appointed Jewish surname), are you missing something?" I pleaded innocent.

"Because an irritated pimp called me over to his table during lunch to show me the used Band Aid he found in his potato salad. I had to 'comp' his meal." Not very inviting fare, was it?

One grease-filled day, when I was a line cook at Ken's in Copley Square, Boston, a burly, disgruntled biker cook took umbrage at the fact that I was promoted to a position he felt was his. The tattooed bad sport responded by swinging a twelve-inch chef's knife at me, catching a finger on my right hand as I held it up for defense, and left the digit swinging in the breeze. It was reattached, but it illustrates what goes on behind the scenes.

I returned to Indiana and began chefing and managing restaurants. During one food-service catering occasion, I met Sandi. Eventually we married and went into the catering business together. On one particular occasion not too many years ago, Sandi and I had just hired Gene, a new cook. He reported the very next day on time, at 8 A.M., but by mid-morning his demeanor drastically changed. His pupils were dilated, indicating the obvious: He was high on something. Sandi and her assistant, Trudy, were in the office when Gene yelled out and ask them to come help him in the kitchen. I was out on a delivery.

Apparently, Gene became verbally abusive to the women, so Sandi immediately called me and told me to get back to the kitchen pronto!

When I arrived, the women were panicked and Gene was rambling and out of his mind on who knows what, wielding an eight-inch, razor-sharp boning knife. As he babbled incoherently, I tried to calm him down. As I slowly inched closer to him, I quickly grabbed the knife out of his hand, only to be surprised when he reached around and whipped out another one just like it from under his belt. As much as I'd like to fix up the story, assigning myself the role of the great protector, alas, it was no contest. Nine-one-one, please.

Since 1982, during which time we've been catering to the tastes of Indiana, we've seen it all—and I do mean all. Regular customers are gold, and every respectable caterer has his or her loyal following of devoted groupies. However, those who can afford caterers are fickle. A caterer is only as good as his last performance, and as we all are aware, bad news travels at the speed of light. One year you're hot, then the next year you're not.

Catering is 99 percent improvisation due to unusual customer requests. More often than not, the catering staff brings the kitchen to a client's garage, sets up shop, and proceeds to tray hors d'oeuvres, plate attractive salads, portion out the entrées, and assemble the beautiful desserts without being seen by the guests. Like great waiters, catering staffers are supposed to be there, but not be there.

One of my regular—and favorite—clients from the affluent Northside once called with childlike glee to tell me that he had just purchased a new gas pig roaster and wanted to hire me to come to his home, set up the grill, and roast a whole pig on the new toy. Sounds simple enough, but have you ever roasted a huge, stiff, seventy-five-pound oinker? It's not pretty, especially if you're a vegetarian.

Regardless, Jerry, my assistant chef at that time, and I began to assemble the space-age rotisserie. It had a control panel containing all sorts of dials, buttons, and warning lights.

When the grill was hot, my client went to his garage and proudly brought out the guest of honor, which we proceeded to impale by running him through with a long, motor-operated steel rod that would keep Porky turning over the fire, ensuring even cooking and basting.

If you've ever roasted a pig, you know that balance is the key to success. If the pig is not impaled properly, it will flop around on the skewer and eventually fall into the fire. End of pig. Adjustments must be made to achieve a smooth rotation. As the piggy begins to cook, the fat runs, the carcass softens up, and the juicy pork can easily fall off the rotisserie and into the ash. That's why you see the professionals wrap their pigs in chicken wire before they are roasted. We did that too.

On that particular hot and rainy evening, a major sporting event was being televised and the party hosts had invited friends over for the match and the upscale pig roast.

The host's teenage son had taken it upon himself to immortalize the evening on video. We ignored him and the rolling thunder, transfixed with the chore at hand. After the pig began to soften up, it did begin to flop and rotate unevenly, so Jerry and I had to remove him to readjust his position. The most convenient place to set the pig down was across the ladder going into the pool. Ah, that's when the trouble began.

Number One Son continued to video as rain began to pour on us. Jerry and I grabbed two trash bags and rapidly cut out holes for our heads and arms and pulled them on. We hadn't yet been paid, so we hung in there, still being our pleasant selves. Business as usual.

Our teenage Fellini, intent on looking for the best angles, accidentally nudged the half-cooked porker off the ladder and into the pool—the deep end. With a trailing plume of grease, the razorback sank into the turquoise, chlorinated water and came to rest ten feet directly below the diving board. The pig had plunged.

We had seen it coming, but it was too late. Everything went into slow motion.

Just then, my client came out to check on how the barbecue was progressing, just in time to witness the "kersplash!" of the evening's main course. Unaffected, he quietly disappeared into the house and returned momentarily in his swimming suit and carrying a bolo grande of red wine. He entered the pool's shallow end, marched into the deep end, sucked in a deep breath, jackknifed, grabbed the pig, surfaced, and handed one end of the pig to me and the other end to Jerry. Meanwhile, rain continued to cascade down and bolts of lightning danced all around us.

"Now what do we do?" I asked. "We will serve no swine before its time," I added, fearful that we were going to take the rap for this debacle. Jerry and I were big drinkers back then, so we had already discretely quaffed down a few beers and found all this quite hilarious. Still, the prospect of having to go home chastised and unpaid was making me nervous.

Assuming our evening was a financial bust, we were ecstatic when the client handed us each a c-note, and whispered, "Put 'er back on the spit and don't tell my guests." Jerry and I did a triple-take, and agreed without hesitation. So as the rain continued to pour, there we were, lightning striking all around, dressed in fifty-gallon, dark green trash bags, cooking a chlorine marinated pig. We drank more beer and looked into the dry house through the large bay windows as high society enjoyed TV sports and cocktails. I said to Jerry, "It doesn't get any better than this."

Catering isn't cheap: after all, the entire restaurant, china, tables, chairs, food, and liquor is being delivered to your house! Catering an off-site social affair requires laborious detailed work. It pays to stay sober while paying hosts and guests imbibe.

Because a caterer would do anything to please a customer, unless you are very strong, it is difficult and sometimes, unavoidable, for the caterer and his assistants to refuse a jovial, generous, intoxicated host, aggressively offering cocktails to you and the staff.

And, when I used to heavily drink, the invitation was a green light on the road to ruin. Catering is a reputation-only business built on word of mouth.

Alcohol can also compromise a host's ability to make rational decisions. One inebriated host, attempting to impress his many guests, boisterously boasted he'd tipped the catering staff of five a thousand dollars. We refused, but he insisted. Of course, the next day, with embarrassment in his voice, he called to request that we return the check. We had expected the call and were glad to refund the overly generous tip.

On at least a dozen occasions, when we arrived to confirm the choreography and menus for a party with people of means, it was interesting to note that the only furnished rooms in the home were the bedroom and kitchen. The living, family, and dining rooms were totally empty. "Our new furniture will be here before the party," the client would venture. We would nod approvingly. After all, there was a Mercedes in the garage and mink coats were in the hall closet.

When we would arrive at the home bearing paraphernalia for the party, the home would be beautifully and miraculously furnished down to the rare assortment of handsome original oil paintings hanging regally on the freshly painted walls.

"Hey, they really bought some nice appointments," I would mention to Sandi, "and they got here right on time, just like they said." But when we went over the next day to pick up the rentals and a check, the furniture and the paintings would have mysteriously disappeared. Acceptance by the social community has its costs, but any wannabe can rent furniture and paintings by walking through the Yellow Pages.

As anyone who is over three years old in the Hoosier capital knows, Indianapolis is the home of the Greatest Spectacle in Racing, the Indy 500.

The most decadent spectacle of flaunted wealth I ever experienced happened one race day in the middle 1980s when a wealthy Indianapolis baron held a "toga" party at his home following the waving of the checkered flag. As the limos pulled up, excited guests exited, decked out in fashionable white robes. The flesh was fresh, tawny, and abundant.

Everyone was in a festive mood, and the alcohol flowed. The smell of Poison perfume and marijuana smoke filled the air.

Limousine after limousine pulled in the circular driveway, dropping off merry revelers at the six-thousand-square-foot mansion, which was done totally in white from the ceiling to the carpet.

After a while, the well-lubricated guests began to slosh the red wine out of the bolo grande onto the beautiful, white, wall-to-wall carpeting. They were putting their cigarettes out in planters and on the carpet, twirling them into the carpet with the tips of their sandals. Oddly enough, when our sincere concerns for the carpet were expressed to the host, he became a little irritated and blithely remarked, "Don't worry about it, it's not your problem, I'll have the carpet replaced tomorrow! Now, get back to my guests."

Catering a wedding is a stressful, awe-inspiring responsibility, as a lifelong memory is being created. No two nuptial parties are alike. An experienced caterer attempts to create an event equal to the dreams and expectations of the bride and her mother, brought to notice through many issues of *Bride* magazine and several cousins' weddings. The caterer can sit amidst a storm of temper tantrums, tears, clashes and disagreements in perception. Dad must pick up the check, and he has his part to play, usually vocally, about expenses.

Money is usually the big issue. In the Midwest, it's difficult to get the average wedding party to spend more than five thousand to ten thousand dollars for a modestly presented wedding reception. However, when I worked for catering customers in Boston, dropping twenty thousand to a hundred thousand for a wedding was normal. Still, all of these festivities are expensive. Nobody elopes, but when the bills come in, they wish they had.

After catering over two hundred weddings, one particular reception, held within the beautiful halls of a building in downtown Indianapolis, has been permanently etched in our minds.

The bride was exhaustingly verbose, controlling, and demanding in arranging the menu and catering choreography for the big event, arguing about every detail of the salad, the pasta dish, and the tablecloths, and making us feel as if we were extorting her for money.

Nevertheless, on the big day, the ceremony went forward and we waited as the by-now hungry guests began to arrive for the reception.

These days, in my opinion, weddings are extravagant pageants of theatrical proportion, planned for the benefit of the leading characters, often too ostentatious, usually beyond the means of those who must pay, and sometimes showing little relationship to the sacredness of the promises a man and woman must make before God. In addition, brides (and grooms sometimes, too) fail to take their guests into consideration while going through the nuptial paces. "This is my day to be princess," says the bride, "and they can dance to my tune." Of course it's your day, I say, but you have invited your friends and relatives to share your joy, so why not consider them too?

On this particular day, the bride and groom decided to take an extra trip around town while the guests impatiently waited for the arrival of the wedding party to herald the beginning of the festivities. The puzzled guests kept glancing at their watches and the alcohol began to kick in as the milling crowd, hungry and bored, grew restless. "Where are they? What's going on? I'm hungry. Can we eat?" However, wedding etiquette requires the presence of the bride and groom to go through the serving line first.

We were also impatient to serve. The kitchen at the reception facility was located in the basement and could be accessed only by using an enormous freight elevator, so we set up a prep station in the elevator to make refilling the buffet more efficient, a real logistical nightmare. It was one of those typical, blisteringly hot and humid Indiana summer afternoons, so by the time we had arrived, the thousand pounds of ice we'd ordered was melting into a one-inch flood in the garage area. We cleaned that up, but the heat was compounding the problem in the reception area.

After a very long and awkward hour of waiting for the bride and groom to show up, several of the guests, emboldened by booze, aggressively assaulted one of the buffet tables in a sharklike frenzy and insulted the caterers in lieu of the tardy bride and groom. Eventually, the wedding party arrived, the unhappy guests began gorging, the music and dancing took off, and, for all intents and purposes, the reception actually turned into a lovely affair.

As the last of the spent guests staggered out the front doors into the muggy summer evening and plopped down in their awaiting automobiles, the bride and groom sneaked off for a quiet moment, behind a large marble pillar, where, I'm sure, they thought their conversation would go unheard. I happened to be nearby, leaning against another pillar, and couldn't help but overhear.

"What do you think? Did we do it?" the fresh bride inquired.

"Yes, definitely, yes! We invited and impressed the right people. This whole thing should boost both of our careers. Good job, baby!" the groom confidently boasted, as he embraced his soul mate.

Using one the most important moments in their lives to enhance their finances and careers might not be the best way to start off a life of marital bliss.

ᕓ

One of the more interesting aspects of our catering business is providing in-flight food service for most of the teams in the National Basketball Association.

In 1990 my catering relationship with the league began. At that time the options for those who managed the teams was bland, chain airline catering, and Joy Woods, the Indiana Pacers' head attendant for the flights, was open to more high quality options.

We tried out, cooking dishes for Joy and the decision-makers and we were on! There were strict parameters: cook "meat-and-potatoes" food, and plenty of it; deliver it on time; don't fawn over the players or converse with them; and get in and out lickity-split.

Going into the in-flight catering business was a shock to our systems. Airplanes have galley areas (you've seen them on commercial planes, of course) where food in pans is taken in, then distributed to individual serving plates at the appropriate moment in flight. That meant that we had to not only purchase huge quantities of the pans and serving dishes but also to be aware of the configuration of the plane—food preparation and service areas are different in a 727 from the same sort of areas in another plane. We ended up buying over 100,000 pans to start our service.

We're an FDA-inspected service, so strict temperature controls prevail when we cook and store food for the NBA flights. After food is prepared and put in pans, it must be stored at 41 degrees until delivered to the plane. Then it is heated in a series of steps at precisely controlled temperatures.

How are menus developed? We supply the management firm with a variety of menu choices and they fax us four-page-long orders for each team. Simple salads, pork tenderloins or chicken fixed in tasty ways, short ribs, salmon, mashed potatoes, and delicious desserts— these are the basics of the menu. Police secure the delivery vehicle prior to delivery.

Five people on our catering team serve thirty-five to forty players, coaches and assistant coaches, spouses and significant others, and the sportswriters traveling with the team.

At the time we first went with the NBA, most teams traveled on their own planes, either owned or leased by the team. Today a major airline provides private jet service for 85–90 percent of NBA teams, and we service all of these teams. The Pacers, of course, remain our personal favorite.

Team owners and the NBA itself treat their players very well and realize travel is boring and tiresome. All these athletes see is airport tarmac and hotel rooms, so making the plane deluxe and entertaining helps keep the players from becoming homesick. Food is extremely important to them. The only time the trainers can actually control what goes into the players' mouths is on these flights.

Traditionally, when we arrive with the food, the flight attendants are on a tight schedule and pushing hard to get the plane ready for the players and for timely take-off. An NBA regulation stipulates that each team must arrive in the city of the team twenty-four hours before the game. One wrong move, and the crew will bite your head off.

There are also unspoken rules. When you cater for the NBA stars, you are supposed to pretend that you've done this a thousand times. Be cool, don't gawk, and never, never ask for autographs. Several times, overly exuberant line-crew members from the Flight Based Operation were literally kicked off the plane for gawking, being in the way, and asking for autographs. It isn't appropriate behavior.

The celebs have individually equipped seats. Each player has his own CD Walkman, his favorite music, Gameboys, treats, magazines, or a favorite book. Most players end up in card games to pass the time.

You haven't lived till you see the bathrooms on the NBA private charters. The lovely attendants are instructed to please by providing men's cologne, only the best reading material, and special toilet paper in the johnny. Most toilet seats are at least six inches higher than those at home, so it's quite a surprise when you have to use one for the first time. Anyone got a stepladder out there?

The owner of the Orlando Magic shares his private plane with the team to help make them feel comfortable on the road. This aircraft at one time had two stand-up mahogany showers and a private bathroom just for Shaquille O'Neal. It pays to be the star.

Most of the planes have a special area reserved for just the coaching staff, set up with a table holding a VCR and TV so they can immediately critique the win or loss. Deluxe quarters for real monetary assets.

After running and sweating like thoroughbreds for four quarters, professional basketball players are high-energy metabolism machines in need of sustenance. By the time they arrive via team bus at the plane following the game, to say they are a hungry bunch would be an understatement. It wasn't uncommon to watch the likes of Rik Smits board the craft, pick up five mini-quiches along with three shrimp and with one slam-dunk, they're history. Gulp!

I've witnessed these towering players board the airplane with bags of fast-food burgers, french fries, buckets of that finger-lickin'-good fried chicken, boxes of Ho-Hos, Ding Dongs, Little Debbie's oatmeal cookies, and candy bars, along with other performance inhibiting delicacies. However, those days are over, now that professional trainers have become aware that there is a direct relationship between food and performance.

As a result of the knowledge we've gained over the years, we who feed the teams know well what foods each individual team requires and how each team prefers to eat. Early on, we began matching their records against what they ate, and we learned that the teams who ate healthily were at the top of their division. So we quietly do our own encouraging of good nutrition habits.

Overall, the healthiest and most conscientious eaters are the teams from the West Coast: Los Angeles, Portland, Seattle, and Sacramento. During the NBA finals play-off battle, we were catering for the Lakers and the Pacers. The Lakers had five vegans and the Pacers two vegetarians.

But there are teams who want the food to be like Mom's: fatty, buttery, plainly adorned, and with gravy. Gravy is okay, but no sauce. "None of that low-fat stuff for us thank you!" Once, only once, I served a salad of romaine, red cabbage, and grated carrots. Simple enough. Then the trainer took a look at the salad, threw it at me, and accused me of attempting to serve gourmet food, as if it were a mortal sin. Sheesh! "We don't want any gourmet food, these guys want what they're used to." What he wanted was a plain iceberg lettuce, tomato, and cucumber salad.

What are you going to tell a nineteen-year-old millionaire who makes five times the coach's salary? Tell him to eat whatever he wants! The food has to be plain, not too fancy, almost homestyle. He just left home, remember?

And then there was one of those nights the New York Knicks were in town. Before each visit, they call us to arrange for some token fruit and veggie trays. They always get their dinners from the famous carnivore's haven, the St. Elmo Steak House, contending that if they don't eat there, they'll lose to the "Billy Bobs," as they call the Hoosiers.

Our crew got inside the plane and began to unpack the order, when the attendant screeched, "Oh, no, he won't drink Sunkist; it's got to be Tropicana." The "he" was center Patrick Ewing. "This has pulp in it. You've got to replace it."

When the cold January wind blows across the tarmac, it numbs you through to the bone as you climb up the rear end of an idling 727 with the ear-splitting, high-decibel whine of the jet engines and the delightful perfume of jet fuel filling your already frozen nostrils.

It's eleven o'clock at night, five below zero, nearby grocery stores are closed, the closest convenience store doesn't carry half-gallons, and the flight attendant is spitting flames and demands. After ranging through four grocery stores on the west side of Indianapolis, we finally turned up several half gallons of pulp-free Tropicana. We arrived just in time to hand it to the attendant as they closed the door and taxied to the runway. What a way to make a living.

When an NBA team arrives in town, the pilots and crew leave the aircraft in the efficient hands of the Flight Based Operation to be cleaned, fueled, and mechanically checked out. The FBO crew removes the dirty china, silverware, and glassware from the team's previous meal, then washes, sanitizes, and returns these items to the plane.

Sometimes the aircraft sits on the tarmac overnight. A 727 is just like an automobile or bus—it can freeze up. One particular February night was colder than usual and the flight crew was late arriving. We sat on the tarmac for an hour waiting for them to arrive. The plane had been locked down and uninhabited for two days in subzero temperatures.

The antsy flight crew, already behind schedule, arrived from their hotels in shuttle vans, and, as usual, we hesitated boarding until they got on the plane, turned on the lights, heat, galley power, and fired up the engines. Aircraft etiquette.

Every team carries a stash of assorted soft drinks, fruit juices, beer, wine, water, and bottled iced tea. So, when the flight crew boarded the dark, cold craft, a cataclysmic, gooey, sticky mess from cockpit to tail greeted them. Frozen bottles throughout the plane had exploded.

Traveling on the road with the team can get boring, so occasionally the younger, more mischievous players will play tricks on each other, just as any other twenty-something males do. Boys will be boys.

Well, it was the first stop on a long West Coast swing when things got out of hand in Phoenix. A young Reggie Miller of the Indiana Pacers decided he'd gather up everyone's overcoats, left on the plane in this warm weather, and, unbeknownst to them, place them in a locker in Phoenix. When a team goes on the road, the press corps, owners, wives, and girlfriends often travel with them; their coats were also held hostage.

Presumably, after the game the players didn't give a thought to their coats and boarded the flight for L.A. After landing they headed to their hotels to check into their rooms and get settled before heading to the arena. As we all know, it is next to impossible to check into any hotel without identification, let alone get past security and into a professional basketball arena without proper press credentials.

The coats! Where are the coats? The majority of the victims carried their important identification and passes in the winter coats, so they were in quite a pickle. No one knew what had taken place and a snickering Reggie never let on. Joy Woods, their on-the-road "mom" and flight attendant was the only one who knew what had transpired in Phoenix and watched the madness unfold, noticing Reggie was doing his best to stifle laughter. Several times Joy told him he better fess up, but Reggie, feeling cute, didn't want to hear it. This was too much fun, and as yet, no one suspected he was behind it.

Eventually, the situation worked itself out, Reggie fessed up, and the charter service took an expensive, unscheduled flight back to Phoenix to get the coats. As I said, boys will be boys.

To help the players feel comfortable, teams usually have the same flight crews throughout the long season away from family, friends, and loved ones. It's pleasant to board an aircraft and be greeted by the familiar, smiling face of a woman who acts as "road mom" while traveling. The regular flight crew also has intimate knowledge of each player's likes and dislikes, and makes every effort to make each player feel happy and comfortable.

This also applies to the flight attendants; over the years we have made dear friends with many of them. Since several of the young women and pilots have flown with the same teams for four to five years, they have become a family. Over the years we couldn't help but make a few great friends, too. It's all hugs and kisses when the flight attendants see us pulling up to the rear of the plane to unload. "How have you guys been? What's new in your life? How are the kids?" After all, they've been on the lonely road away from friends and loved ones too. They tell us that they too are tired of seeing tarmac, sleeping in sterile hotel rooms, and eating lousy hotel food.

Sandi and I celebrate Thanksgiving by renting a secluded log cabin on a pumpkin farm in Noblesville, Indiana. It is an authentic log house with no electricity or running water, and just a potbelly stove for heat. It's a wonderfully romantic way to celebrate Thanksgiving: no television or radio to distract quality conversation. We make cowboy coffee on the potbelly stove, build a bonfire outside, and keep warm by snuggling with each other.

There's always a basketball game the night before or the day of Thanksgiving, so the stewardesses are left to fend for themselves back at the hotel. We have, on occasion, invited them to join us in our family celebration. It usually takes a millisecond for them to excitedly accept the invitation to join us in our family feast, and all of a sudden, it's not so lonely on the road. We flew to Austin, Texas, to attend the wedding of Joy Woods, the flight attendant who got us started with the NBA. To this day, she and her husband are very special friends. A nice perk!

The Miami Heat, with coach Pat Riley, come to Indianapolis twice annually, and when they do, they call us to prepare their meals. It took a long time to earn their business away from the competition, but eventually we took hold. Kathy, their head flight attendant, calls us several days in advance with the menu. We're the grocery store of the sky and the Stuckey's of the airways, ambassadors of culinary excellence who want everyone who flies out of Indy to leave with a good taste, so to speak, in their mouths.

On one occasion, Kathy called us as usual to order preflight hors d'oeuvres, veggie and fruit trays, shrimp cocktails, crab legs, and dinner entrées for the entire crew. Upon delivery check-in, Kathy looked at Sandi and inquired, "Where's the soup, and how come there's only one filet mignon dinner? I need eleven of them."

"Kathy," Sandi replied, beginning to squirm, "we're sorry, but you didn't order soup and you ordered only one filet mignon dinner." The customer is always right, right?

Kathy, under tremendous pressure, blew up and demanded we come up with some soup and another ten filet dinners quickly.

We flew down the steps of the craft, into our van, and took off on a mission: Hot soup for forty-five and another ten filet dinners. Not an easy assignment at eleven o'clock at night. After frantically driving around we landed at Denny's, ran in, asked for the manager, explained our situation, and asked for help. "No problem," he assured us. Whew!

The next thing we knew, the manager walked out with a huge

plastic container of soup, frozen solid. It would take a fairly large and powerful microwave to melt through such a mass; we didn't have the time, but we had no choice. The flight was leaving in forty-five minutes. Meanwhile, while the soup was being nuked, we asked him if he had any beef tenderloin steaks on hand, "We need ten dinners with mashed potatoes and fresh vegetables." Again, "No problem."

We plopped at the counter and waited, and waited, and waited for what felt like an eternity. Finally, with no time to spare, we drove like maniacs through the tarmac gates and to the plane, did the hand-off, and they were off.

Kathy called back and thanked us for our effort and placed another order for the next week when they'd be back again. This time, we had a new chef in the kitchen, a deviation from the norm. I usually do all the food preparation myself. Believe me when I say that there are multitudes of people out in the restaurant world who love to call themselves chefs, but they can't even fry chicken. They can cook the fancy stuff, but haven't a clue when it comes to basic fundamentals. And it is basic stuff, cooked superbly, that the NBA likes.

We had a large Christmas party going out that evening so I asked the new chef to put together the Miami order. It wasn't very complicated, but he managed to screw it up royally. The food was delivered and we thought everything was okey-dokey. The next day I got a call from Kathy telling me that "Coach Riley said it was the worst meal he'd ever eaten." My heart sank. We "comped" the meal and apologized all over ourselves, and said to ourselves, "Well, we'll never hear from them again."

Next season Sandi and I noticed on the schedule that the Heat were coming to town soon and lamented how we surely had lost that account. I was wrong. We were dumfounded when Kathy called. She said Coach Riley had told her to "Give that man another chance." We gratefully complied, and Kathy called back the next day to say that the coach said it was the best meal he'd had on a flight in years. My esteem for Coach Riley rose and I learned a valuable lesson: Everyone deserves a second chance.

〜

CHAPTER ELEVEN

Food Safety — Preventing Food-Borne Illness

As the stomach turns—or when bad food happens to good people.

A beautiful cool crisp evening, the cobalt skies so clear you can reach out and run your fingers through the stars. Tiff and Mark just savored a magnificent meal, a fruity but dry glass of wine, wonderful conversation, coffee and a warming cognac at their favorite bistro, and are fully enjoying a leisurely romantic after-dinner walk, when all of a sudden, out of nowhere, it happens—the urge to purge.

"What's wrong? Something you ate?" Tiffany asks. "It couldn't be. That's the hippest new place in town and the chef is so well-known." This may appear to be a little melodramatic but it is frighteningly accurate and it happens every day, millions of times a year at even the finest of restaurants, with the best chefs directing the action. The twisted plot line in this soap opera is "kitchen integrity."

Since salmonella and *E. coli* take several days to "cook," Marc more than likely came down with an ugly little case of staphylococcal intoxication. These bacteria are found on the skin and in the nose and throat of most people; and people with colds and sinus infections are special carriers. Symptoms appear one to eight hours after eating the bug and generally last for several days. Mark may remember his meal for a long time.

The Johns Hopkins Medical Newsletter advises us to make a connection with a doctor immediately after acquiring food-borne illness. A delayed diagnosis can allow a mass outbreak to occur, if the source of infection is the public food supply rather than a food contamination at home.

By the way, there is a board of health ruling in most states that mandates that if an employee has a fever, sore throat, diarrhea, vomiting, or jaundice, she or he must report to the person-in-charge. When these issues are reported to the manager on duty, they should exclude and restrict those employees from the establishment or keep them from working with exposed food, clean utensils, equipment, linen, and unwrapped single service and single-use articles.

Does the kitchen have a collective conscience? Do they wash the field and pesticide residue from the produce before it becomes your Caesar salad? Do they keep raw chicken, beef, fish, and pork at safe temperatures during storage to prevent increased bacterial activity? Do they cook their meats and eggs to the proper temperatures to sufficiently destroy harmful pathogens? Have the mushrooms been washed since they were pulled out of the dark, loamy, manure medium? Do they remove chemical cleansing agents from utensil and beverage surfaces?

Our friends at the Center for Disease Control in Atlanta recently quantified the impact of food-borne diseases on health in the United States. Nibble on these findings: Each year in America there are approximately 76 million food-related illnesses, 325,000 hospitalizations and 5,000 deaths. Sounds like statistics from a bloody Third World insurrection.

From the farm to the fork, we give precious little attention to the cleanliness and safety practices of the food we consume and the restaurants we frequent. We go to restaurants to relax, have a good time, avoid cooking at home, not to freak out and check to see that the employees are washing their hands.

Whom can we trust? Can we eat out without doubt or do we dine at our own risk? Did I just hear a sneeze from the cook who is composing my salad? Does the management monitor the food-handling practices of the employees? Did the server wash his hands

Is There a Doctor in the Kitchen?

Washing your hands after working with raw poultry can prevent salmonella. The U.S. Centers for Disease Control and Prevention reports that salmonella typhimurium, which accounts for at least 24 percent of all reported salmonella cases, is growing increasingly drug-resistant.

"In the past six or seven years this subtype has grown from being about 7 percent of all salmonella typhimurium isolates that we've tested to almost 40 percent," says Dr. Jeremy Sobel of the CDC's Division of Bacterial and Mycotic Diseases.

Hand washing procedures:
- Wet hands with water as hot as the hands can comfortably stand.
- Apply one tablespoon of soap and lather to elbow.
- Create friction by rubbing hands for twenty to thirty seconds.
- Cover all surfaces on hands and wrists, around and under fingernails, around rings, and as high up on arms as possible.
- Rinse thoroughly under running water.
- Dry with paper towels or hot air dryer.
- Turn off faucets and other possible contaminated surfaces with paper towels.
- Always wash hands thoroughly before returning to food preparation activities.

Special note: Keep a mild solution of bleach water near the food prep area. Use about a capful per two quarts of water. Store your cleaning sponges and towels there; then they are ready to wipe off counters, door handles, phone receivers, and anything with which you might have come in contact. Change and refresh the bleach water daily.

after using the toilet? Was the lime in my cocktail washed before being plunged into my drink, was the pork left out at room temperature too long, and were the salad greens properly cleaned? Is the guy grinding fresh hamburger from England, is the chef sleeping with the salad girl, and does the broiler cook have Ebola?

Are you aware that the produce so beautifully displayed at the market was sprayed with pesticides and fungicides, coated with field residue, packaged unwashed or sanitized and shipped, for your convenience, directly to the grocery chain? Some fairly disgusting things can happen to produce in the field during the growing process. Animals, birds, bacteria, and mold can venture onto the products, to mention only a few disgusting consequences.

E. coli and salmonella can also be acquired by eating watermelon, raspberries, cabbage, or any produce grown on or near the ground. Perhaps a migrant worker had hepatitis or changed a baby's soiled diaper while out in the fields.

In Greenwood, Indiana, a batch of coleslaw infected customers with *E. coli*. Through tracking and proper documentation it was discovered that a cabbage farmer in Texas was adjacent to a cattle ranch. One day the roaming cattle trampled the fences of the cabbage farm, made themselves at home, and for a short period of time, proceeded to engage in a cabbage festival. Without getting disgusting, the cattle left a lot of residue during the process, leaving some of the cabbage colonized with *E. coli* bacteria.

Salmonella, on the other hand, is generally associated with consumption of chickens that were not cooked to the proper interior temperature of 165 degrees. Factory farm chickens are the most contaminated due to the pathetically filthy and inhumane growing conditions. Go on-line and tap into "factory farms" and get the scoop. When you do that, you'll also learn about how to support the family farm which is so important to our country's character and future.

It is in our nature to turn the channel and surf into denial and quickly blame our nausea and discomfort on the stomach flu, but the hard cold facts are that it was the dinner. Denial can get us into trouble. Food always has been, and always will be, dangerous. Remember, de Nile is in Egypt, and de pharaohs are dead.

So what do we do? Stop eating out? A resounding NO! There are hoards of great restaurants practicing safe food handling techniques. Unfortunately, bad news travels much faster than good news.

Indiana has the answer.

John Livengood, president of the Restaurant and Hospitality Association of Indiana, recently championed Senate Bill 404, the most important food safety legislation that has come before the Indiana General Assembly in the eleven years he has represented the food industry. It simply states that each licensed Indiana restaurant must have someone in each restaurant on a daily basis who is trained and certified in food safety. Livengood feels strongly that it will do more to protect the public against food-borne illness than anything else we can do. "It will increase voluntary compliance with food safety laws and decrease the need for enforcement through regulation and multiple inspections. Plus, it will save valuable tax dollars for other public needs," Livengood states.

Over the twenty-five years of being involved in the food and service industry, I have witnessed some vile behavior, more than I would like to admit. For example, chefs moving produce straight from the field-packed box to the skillet without washing; cooked chicken breasts dropped on the floor, then back on the plate; servers nibbling on your dinner; and uncovered sneezing over freshly prepared food. There's more, but good taste prevents me from continuing. Just take my word for it: What this really becomes is an exercise in kitchen values.

The restaurant and hotel industry has afforded me the best experiences, memories, and friendships of my life. It is my life, it's how I met my wife, but, as anyone who has ever worked in a professional kitchen will tell you, there is an unseen dark side to what goes on "Behind the Kitchen Doors." I've always felt that everyone across the USA needs to work in a restaurant just once, to truly understand what happens before your beautifully prepared meal is plopped down in front of you and your family.

 ❧

Here is some food for thought when you eat out:

Were the lemons or limes washed before they were sliced for your tea or cocktail? You might check to see if you see dirt spots.

Before it is filled, hold your water or wine glass up to the light to get a good view of the glass. You'd be surprised.

Are there spots on the silverware? Look at the knife.

Does the server have dirty fingernails? Does he or she wash hands regularly during the shift after handling money and soiled dishes during the shift?

Is the exhibition kitchen staffed with long-haired broiler cooks? Is everyone wearing a hair restraint?

Are the bathrooms clean? If they're dirty, then you can be guaranteed that the kitchen is dirty as well.

If you can summon the courage, ask your server if the produce was properly cleaned before it was transformed into a plate of edible art.

If those little black things in the corner aren't chocolate-covered raisins, then you're probably seeing rodent droppings. Dead insects indicate poor cleaning. If you happen to observe rodent droppings, mousetraps, or bait in an obscure corner, just keep on truckin' to the next eating establishment.

Want to have some fun? The next time you go out to dinner, just ask the waitress if the kitchen practices the "Three-Second Rule." In other words, if a food preparation person drops something on the floor—maybe your entrée—the universal kitchen joke is, "Hey, I picked it up within three seconds. It's okay, right?" The kitchen staff laughs and mumbles indifferently, "Sure, no problem." It's the old "what they don't see won't hurt them" justification. Very common.

And finally, if you do have an enjoyable, nausea free dinner, don't forget to tip your server for the fine job. The term tips means "To Insure Prompt Service." Many diners seem to think tipping is a city in China. That's Tai Ping.

Live by this rule: If you have any reservations, don't make reservations.

When in doubt, check it out. Invite the general manager to your table; ask questions to let that person know your concerns. You'll do more good than harm in increasing his awareness level. To be sure, call your local board of health and obtain records of the establishments inspections.

Waiter! Check please!

Stimulating the immune system

From childhood on, wisdom dictates that it is prudent to evaluate everything we put into our mouths. Sounds logical, especially when it affects our most prized possession, our health.

When I was a child, my mother used to tell us we got sick because we left the window open and "In-flu-enza." Today, all we have to do is shake someone's hand, baby-sit the grandchildren, or be exposed to a biological warfare contaminant.

What can we do? When flu and cold season is here in full force our weakened immune system can fall prey to the flu bug, a bad cold, a nasty little bacteria du jour, or worse, and I am reminded of a famous quote by Hippocrates who once stated, "If you feed a cold, you will have to starve a fever." The reasoning is that if your body is busy with digestion it does not have enough energy for fighting off germs. So, sometimes it is best to go on a modified fast drinking lots of fruit and vegetable juices.

My friend and consultant, Peg Daly, a family nurse practitioner at the Complementary Medicine Center in Greenwood, Indiana, recently informed me that "There is still the threat of a pandemic any year, even with the delay in the flu vaccine production. It is felt every year, that new viral strains from Asia could be a potential concern. Adults the age of thirty-five or older, particularly those approaching sixty to seventy years of age, are more vulnerable to infections due to the thymus gland's decline of specialized T-cells that help strengthen our body's immune system." Peg also supports the fact that we must incorporate foods and supplements with antioxidant properties, along with added zinc, vitamin C, beta-carotene, and echinacea with goldenseal, which will give your body the edge it needs to stay healthy this season. Bolster your immune system by what you eat! In a way, chefs are the doctors of the future.

Seven Steps To Getting Well Sooner

1. When you are sick, wash towels and bedding each day. Add some eucalyptus oil to the wash to get rid of "bed bugs."
2. After you use the thermometer, clean it with rubbing alcohol before replacing it into its sheath.
3. Wash your hands after you sneeze or blow your nose.
4. Use disinfectant on objects around the home you use frequently, such as the telephone, refrigerator door handles, computer keyboard, and desk-drawer pulls.
5. Use disposable tissues as opposed to hankies, which can become a breeding ground for bacteria.
6. Keep your fingers out of your eyes, nose, and mouth. These are the main entry points for germs to get into your system.
7. If available, sit in a steam room to open up clogged nasal passages. You can do this at home by simply filling a bowl with steaming hot water, tenting your head with a towel over the bowl, and breathing in deeply. Add some eucalyptus or mint oil for a refreshing lung treatment. Eucalyptus is great for breaking up sinus and chest congestion, and its antibacterial components make it a good infection fighter. Mix ten to twelve drops in an ounce of a carrier oil, such as almond, sesame, or jojoba, and massage into sinus or chest areas to open up breathing passages.

Drug-Free Remedies

Slippery Elm is the main ingredient in over-the-counter cough medicines. It helps by cleaning out irritating mucus and contains mucilage, a water-soluble fiber that coats and soothes the throat.

Aromatic fresh ginger is a warming spice which can be brewed as a tea to relieve the chills and muscle aches that accompany the flu. It tastes even better when a bit o' honey is added. Take about an inch of fresh ginger, peel it, then smash it with the side of a knife. Place into a tea cup, pour hot water over it, then let it steep for five to ten minutes. Enjoy. Ginger is also helpful in controlling nausea.

The general favorite, garlic, contains a constellation of natural antibiotics, is a general system stabilizer, an immunity booster, and an antioxidant. You can eat it raw if you dare, cooked, or as deodorized capsules or liquid extracts. Garlic has been shown to kill several types of bacteria and viruses.

The granddaddy of flu-foiling remedies is the homeopathic remedy called oscillococcinum (pronounced *uh-SILL-oh-kox-SIGH-num*). Many people swear that it works by stopping the flu symptoms in their tracks, but it must be taken at the first onset of flu symptoms.

Vitamin C is also a trusted ally in combating cold and flu symptoms. One's need for vitamin C goes up dramatically when a cold or the flu is imminent. Take vitamin C at the first signs of symptoms.

Echinacea is also most effective when taken at the first sign of symptoms. If you take one dropperful of the tincture or two capsules three to four times a day for up to five days, your bout with the flu will be less debilitating.

Your body produces mucus in order to flush out viruses and bacteria. Actually, taking over-the-counter antihistamines to dry up your tender, stuffy little nose can prolong the flu. Imagine that. You need to increase the flow of mucus secretions. Drink copious amounts of herbal tea, brewed from licorice, ginger, anise, or fennel seeds, to both increase mucus flow and to thin the mucus. Simmer one teaspoon of these ingredients for ten minutes, strain, and add honey.

VEGETABLE CURE-ALLS

Crisosto Pena, a Mexican Apache, believed that chiles could cure just about anything. He told his daughter I. M. Cirsosto, the great-great-granddaughter of Geronimo, that it was packed full of vitamins and was therefore a cure-all, especially for colds. The story has come to me.

One day Crisosto returned from work and found his wife and five children in bed with the flu. He felt so bad for them that he took out the bag of hot chile pods and soaked them in hot water for fifteen minutes, then put them into a grinder and ground them with the water they were soaked in. He gave each one of his family members a spoonful with a piece of tortilla. About one hour later the family was moving about. The children were out playing, and his wife was cooking dinner.

In Japan, the shiitake mushroom is the "monarch of the mushrooms," and was once so prized that it was reserved especially for only the emperor and his immediate family. The meaty tasting woodland mushroom has been used for centuries for increasing vitality, improving the circulation, and fighting the common cold. Shiitake extracts have been approved for adjuncts to cancer therapy because of their ability to strengthen the immune system during chemotherapy. Some compounds discovered in the shiitake mushroom have successfully lowered cholesterol in animals and humans. The "king of mushrooms" is a rich source of complex carbohydrates, called polysaccharides, which are purported to bolster the immune system. The royal court of Japan believed that they slowed the aging process. In ancient times, the mushroom was regarded as an aphrodisiac. Fungus anyone?

It all boils down to being a bad host. No flu can reside in your body unless you put out the welcome mat by not eating the proper foods, taking supplements, and getting proper exercise. A good mental attitude is also helpful; filling your consciousness with joy and helpfulness and love of your fellow man cannot hurt you! You don't catch diseases, you permit them to become active.

Feeling good and staying healthy all winter, especially when we are kissing and shaking hands with everyone at the many holiday soirees we will attend each season, requires fighting back by making your body an inhospitable host and by practicing prevention as a strategy.

Our creator designed perfect bodies to be on constant alert, prepared to go to war from the time we are born till we die. Our immune cells depend on us for good nutrition in order to have the ammo to defend us against all unwelcome invaders that make us ache, sneeze, wheeze, cough, shiver, and sometimes die. It's all a part of healthful living—and healthful thinking.

The human body is a wonderfully complex system that responds to whatever we eat, drink, inhale, think, and do, just as powerfully as it would a drug, since we are one gigantic bio-chemical factory ourselves. Beauty, feeling good, and staying healthy start from within with a properly functioning immune system and sound life.

There are many simple and easy methods to keep our "healing power" from within revved up and working at maximum capacity to protect us from each year's nasty little crop of cold and flu viruses. We can all lengthen our odds of surviving a biological or germ warfare attack if we eat a plant-based diet which will support proper and effective immune function.

SENSIBLE FOOD SAFETY TIPS

Temperature Guides

Food safety experts agree that foods are properly cooked when they are heated for a long enough time and at a high enough temperature to kill the harmful bacteria that causes food-borne illness. Below are proper cooking temperatures for raw food.

Poultry:
    Chicken .... 165 degrees
    Ground Chicken .... 165 degrees
    Duck .... 165 degrees
    Turkey (unstuffed)... 165 degrees
    Ground Turkey .... 165 degrees
Pork:
    Chops, roasts, ribs:
        medium .... 165 degrees
        well-done .... 170 degrees
    Ham (fresh)............. 160 degrees
    Sausage, fresh .... 160 degrees
Beef:
    Roasts and steaks
        medium-rare .... 145 degrees
        medium .... 160 degrees
        well-done .... 170 degrees
    Ground Beef .... 165 degrees
Eggs:
    Fried or Poached ..... till yolk and white are firm
    Casseroles .... 160 degrees
    Sauces and custards 160 degrees

Cross-contamination is the scientific word for how bacteria can be spread from one food product to another. This is especially true when handling raw meat, poultry, and seafood, so keep these foods and their juices away from ready-to-eat foods.

Separate raw meat, poultry, and seafood from other foods in your grocery shopping cart and your refrigerator. If possible, use a different cutting board for raw meat products.

Always wash hands, cutting boards, dishes, and utensils with hot soapy water after they come in contact with raw meat, poultry, and seafood.

Never place cooked food on a plate that previously held raw meat, poultry, or seafood.

Use a clean meat thermometer, which measures the internal temperature of cooked foods, to make sure meat, poultry, casseroles, and other foods are cooked throughout.

Cook ground meats, where bacteria can spread during processing, to an internal temperature of at least 165 degrees. The CDC links eating undercooked ground beef with a higher risk of illness. Always check the doneness of your ground beef with a thermometer.

Cook eggs until the yolk and white are firm. Do not use recipes in which eggs remain raw or only partially cooked.

Fish should be opaque and easily flake with a fork.

When cooking in a microwave oven, make sure there are no cold spots in food, where bacteria can survive. For best results, cover food, stir, and rotate for even cooking. If there is no turntable, rotate the dish by hand once or twice during cooking.

Bring sauces, soups, and gravies to a boil when reheating. Heat other leftovers thoroughly to at least 165 degrees.

Refrigerate foods quickly because cold temperatures keep harmful pathogens from growing and multiplying. Set your refrigerator control no higher than 40 degrees and the freezer unit at zero. Check temperatures occasionally with an appliance thermometer.

Refrigerate or freeze perishables, prepared foods, and leftovers within two hours or sooner.

Never defrost food at room temperature. Thaw food in the refrigerator, under cold running water, or in the microwave. Marinate foods in the refrigerator.

Divide large amounts of leftovers into small, shallow containers for quick cooling in the refrigerator. Don't pack the refrigerator. Cool air must circulate to keep food safe.

Helpful Resources

CancerNet
This site outlines risk factors, prevention measures, and treatment options for all types of cancer.
www.cancernet.nci.nih.gov

National Institute of Diabetes and Digestive and Kidney Diseases
The NIDDK gives the latest on all the health issues diabetics face, including weight control.
www.niddk.nih.gov

Eden Foods
888-424-eden
www.edenfoods.com

Spectrum Naturals
800-995-2705
www.spectrumorganic.com

Colavita Olive Oil
800-665-4734
www.colavita.com

DrSoy Soy Nuts
800-700-8986
www.drsoy.com

Earthbound Farm
888-eat-organic
www.ebfarm.com

Boca Burgers
www.bocaburger.com

Frey Premium Wines
Organic and Sulfite free wines
800-760-3739
www.freywine.com

Joyva Corporation
718-497-0170

Safe Drinking Water Hot Line
1-800-426-4791
www.epa.gov/safewater

Nasoya Foods
800-229-tofu
www.nasoya.com

Vitasoy USA, Inc.
800-vitasoy
www.vitasoy-usa.com

The Environmental Defense Fund
An Eco-Scorecard
They put the power of the environmental action at your fingertips.
    Search by geographic area, company name, or use regional maps
    to pinpoint pollution offenders in your area.
www.Scorecard.org

Natural Investor
Visit the natural investor to find out recent stock quotes for the
    natural products industry.
www.naturalinvestor.com

American Heart Association
Information on exercising and nutrition, as well as healthy recipes.
www.amhrt.org

Health Finder
Created by the U.S. Dept. of Health and Human Services. Provides
links to online publications, databases, and medical web sites.
www.healthfinder.gov

Environmental Nutrition
A newsletter of food, nutrition, and health
www.environmentalnutritition.com

Mayo Clinic
A library with news updates, health quizzes, and an "Ask Mayo"
feature for querying a Mayo physician or dietician.
www.mayohealth.org

On Health
A fun general health site with daily news updates and health tips,
access to medical advisers, and discussion areas.
www.onhealth.com

Your Health
Information for staying healthy, from recipes to a section for
querying online health experts.
www.yourhealth.com

Family Doctor
Consult the family doctor. In this case, the American Academy of
Family Physicians Web site.
www.familydoctor.org

Organic Farming
Get down to earth with the Organic Farming Research Foundation.
Examine the latest results on organic farming practices then check
out the schedule of events and farming conferences.
www.Ofrf.org

Around the Kitchen
Looking for a copy of that dog-eared cookbook that your grandma
used when she created her fresh tomato sauce? Track down rare
and out-of-print cookbooks and food-related ephemera.
www.Aroundthekitchen.com

Eco Scorecard
The Environmental Defense Fund puts the power of environmental
action at your fingertips. Search by geographical area, company
name, or use regional maps to pinpoint pollution offenders in
your area. For no charge they will fax your protest to big
polluters and e-mail state and federal decision makers.
www.scorecard.org

The Natural Investor
Visit the natural investor to find out recent stock quotes for the
natural products industry.
www.naturalinvestor.com

Analyze This
Want to analyze your meals for their nutritional content?
www.Global-fitness.com/nat/mainnat.htm

Journal of Nutrition
Published by the American Society of Nutritional Sciences.
www.nutrition.org

Vegan Outreach
An international organization dedicated to furthering vegetarian
living and an improved environment.
www.veganoutreach.org

Mother Nature's General Store
Feel free to browse the contents of their online bookstore and run
customized searches by topic or media type. Search for answers
about natural health care.
www.mothernature.com

Viva Veggie Society
This group gets the message out by distributing information about
vegetarianism to pedestrians on busy street corners.
Contains "101 Reasons Why I am a Vegetarian."
www.earthbase.org/vivaveggie/index/html

Healthy Diets for Dogs
Why should your dog eat lousy canned foods when you can buy
organics?
Shows dog lovers how to cook for their pets and keep current on the
latest medical research.
www.robustokitchens.com

Health and Nutrition—God's Word for the Biblically Inept
ISBN 0-914984-05-5
www.starburstpublishers.com

The Garlic Store
There is no better way to detox from winter's excesses than with
the "stinking rose." A one-stop shop for hundreds of garlic
recipes, tools, specialty foods, garlic flowers, and gifts.
www.garlicstore.com

Index of Recipes